D0991533

Richard Parkes Bonington

Self-portrait. Oil. 1825-6.

RICHARD PARKES
BONINGTON

Carlos Peacock

R P Bonington

TAPLINGER PUBLISHING COMPANY
NEW YORK

First published in the United States in 1980 by
Taplinger Publishing Co., Inc.
New York, New York

Printed in Great Britain

Library of Congress Catalog Card Number: 79-63955
ISBN 0-8008-6793-9

CONTENTS

ACKNOWLEDGEMENTS

The author would like to express his thanks to the following owners and institutions for permission to reproduce works from their collections. (Colour plates are indicated by Roman numerals, monochrome by page reference.)

Thomas Agnew & Sons Ltd I, IV, VII, IX, 32, 41, 53, 83, 84, 89, 95; The Art Gallery of Western Australia, Perth XII; Ashmolean Museum, Oxford 51 (top); Reproduced by Courtesy of The Trustees of The British Museum 35, 37, 38 (top and bottom), 42 (left), 70, 74, 80, 99; Christie's XVII; City Museum & Art Gallery, Nottingham XI, XX, 22, 75, 92; The Covent Garden Gallery III and jacket (front); Garmon Ryan Collection, Walsall 42 (right), 82; Little Gallery, London 29; Musée du Louvre, Paris XVIII, 60, 91; National Trust, Anglesey Abbey, Cambridge X; Earl of Shelburne 15, 31, 58, 61, 62, 63, 69, 71, 72, 94; Tate Gallery, London V; Victoria and Albert Museum, London, Crown Copyright XVI; Reproduced by permission of the Trustees of the Wallace Collection VIII, XII, XIV, XIX; William Weston Gallery, London 101, 102; The Whitworth Art Gallery, Manchester II; Yale Center for British Art 43, 55

The remainder of the pictures are from private collections.

Photographic acknowledgements

Clichés Musées Nationaux, Paris XVII, 60, 91; John R. Freeman & Co. (Photographers) Ltd. VIII, XII, XIV, XIX; Layland Ross Ltd. XI, XX, 22, 75, 92; Tom Scott VI.

LIST OF ILLUSTRATIONS

COLOUR

MONOCHROME

FOREWORD

IF BONINGTON were alive today, his success would ensure that we knew everything about him. We should know his political views, his theories of art, his mode of life, his plans and aspirations for the future. He would be 'featured', as the phrase goes, in the coloured supplements of newspapers and in the glossy magazines. And inevitably there would be photographs of him working on some painting in his Paris studio.

As it is, we know practically nothing of him: a few dates; a few facts; some plausible conjectures; a grain or two of legend. From these and from the art itself we have to gather what clues we can to the personality and achievement of this brilliant product of the Romantic movement. That we have so little precise knowledge of him may seem less surprising when we remember that art in Bonington's time did not have the news value that it has today, that he died extremely young, and that many of his closest friends were still (as he himself virtually was) at that student stage when records for posterity seem of little importance compared with the crowding sensations of the present.

There is a tendency when we find our knowledge of some famous person to be limited or incomplete to assume that this particular person was an enigmatic figure. Thus we might be tempted to label Jane Austen or Bonington as enigmas. In Bonington's case (and we may safely say in Jane Austen's too) all the evidence points to an openness of character, a direct and uninhibited response to life which leaves little room for doubts and contradictions.

It was this extrovertive quality in Bonington which charmed Delacroix from the start and helped to counteract the sense of loneliness that sometimes tortured him. And there was another trait in Bonington which attracted Delacroix – a taste for fashionable clothes which appealed to that side of the Frenchman which liked to play the dandy. Perhaps, too, his professional interest in the artistic effects of draperies on the human figure gave him a critical eye for clothes in general.[1] When, for instance, he visited England in 1825, he was struck by what he called 'a general shabbiness', and he found the women 'all slovenly, with dirty stockings and clumsy shoes'. But if contact with Bonington helped to some extent to persuade Delacroix that the English were not always clad in drab and clumsy clothes, his meeting later in Paris with the great J. M. W. Turner, painter of golden mists and ethereal light, must have provided the final disenchantment. 'I was not particularly impressed', Delacroix records in his journals; 'he looked like an English farmer with his rough black coat and heavy boots . . .'

Anyone who writes about Bonington's work will sooner or later find himself confronted with problems of chronology and style. The very nature of his talent makes it so, for his art came to him so readily that it seems almost irrelevant to speak of stages of development. Overnight, so to speak, the boy artist became a mature and accomplished painter, a master of water-colour technique, and gifted with a kind of prescient knowledge that dictated the form his art should take.

Constable once said that it was the landscape of his native Stour Valley that made him an artist, and it might be said perhaps with equal truth that it was the ports and shipping of the English Channel that gave Bonington a compulsive urge to paint. But between the two, however, there is a notable difference. With Constable the environment that inspired him was something he had been born and bred in; with Bonington the creative stimulus of the sea and its life came to him suddenly and at a particularly impressionable age. In his case, born as he was in the English land-locked Midlands, and living at a time when transport was expensive and difficult, the chances that he had ever seen the sea before the Bonington family sailed for Calais in the autumn of 1817 are remote indeed. To a boy of fifteen what a revelation the first sight of the Channel must have been: the ships riding there at anchor or with sails spread; the smell of tar; the creak of planks and tackle; the sea blue and sparkling round the white cliffs. Under the impact of these things the rudimentary talent for art which the boy possessed made its first rapid stride towards maturity. Small wonder then that when the Bonington family settled down to the lace-making trade in Calais, with all the life and colour of the port on their doorstep, young Bonington preferred to wander about the quays sketching the shipping there instead of devoting himself to the drudgery of lace-designing as his father intended.

Now when we think of Bonington's work we tend automatically to conjure up visions of coast scenes, shipping on sunlit seas, rivers silvery in the morning light, stretches of heath where the clear reds and blues of peasant costumes glow against a pearly distance. It is all so luminous, so sure of touch that it seems in some way self-created.

Though Bonington sometimes used sketches as the basis for his larger work, he was not so dependent on them as Constable. He would paint from direct observation or from memory with an equal degree of freshness, and it was part of his special gift that he was able to combine vigour and breadth of technique with a quality that one might define as studio refinement. As an architectural draughtsman, too, he could be as detailed and accurate as anyone. In his early days this proved an invaluable asset, earning him money that helped to pay for his first sketching tour. At this time he used to hire a cab, and there, safely sheltered from plaguing urchins and the noises and distractions of the Paris streets, he would settle down to do those sketches of the city which earned him fifteen or twenty francs a piece.

But even these early efforts had a distinction about them that instantly caught the eye. And the personal nature of their style seems to have acted as a challenge to other artists to try to work in the same manner. There is a story told that when Bonington was studying under Baron Gros in Paris a fellow student painted a picture in a style so close to Bonington's that Bonington mistook the picture for one of his own. It is a difficult story to believe, but the basis of it may be that the good-natured Bonington made a pretence of being deceived in order to please some student that he liked.

This copying of Bonington's style which began here in a light-hearted, student way went on in various forms for a hundred years at least. One might say that it became a major occupation in the artistic world of the nineteenth century. It varied from works painted deliberately to deceive, to the oils and water-colours done by men whose admiration for Bonington inspired them to follow his manner as closely as they could. There were also what one might call borderline copyists, the artist's father being one. After Bonington's death, his father lived comfortably by selling his son's work in a series of carefully timed sales. He even went so far as to bully French owners into giving him back the Boningtons they possessed. When the supply of Boningtons began to run dry, old Bonington would fill out a thin sale by slipping in works of his own done in his son's manner. In later years when these works reappeared they were often mistaken for genuine examples of Bonington's work and sold as such.

But the real difficulty of identification comes with those artists who were so close to Bonington in spirit and feeling that their work is almost identical with his. Take, for example, an architectural subject by John Scarlett Davis, a Paris scene by Thomas Shotter Boys, an early oil sketch of Venice by William Callow – the closeness of such works to Bonington's is a warning against being too certain of what is by him and what is not. And the difficulties are increased by all the French followers – by Francia, by Paul Huet (the artist who claimed that in his student days he had deceived Bonington with a painting of his own) by Eugène Isabey, Victor Dupré and others.

Among the English followers there is one who deserves some special mention, though he was a follower of Bonington for only a limited period of his life: David Cox. In 1829 Cox went to Calais, and it seems that the associations of Bonington with that ancient port moved him to paint very much in the Bonington manner, to produce during his French tour a wonderful series of water-colours, remarkable for their delicate pencil work and their purity of tone. After this visit to France, Cox never again came under the Bonington spell, and this group of drawings remains unique among his work.

FOREWORD

That Bonington is not better known as an artist is the fault of fate. Had he lived another twenty years or so, his paintings would not be the rarities that they now are on gallery walls. As it is, we must reckon ourselves fortunate that in the eleven or twelve years of his creative life he produced works that stand among the masterpieces of his time. Inevitably, over the years the names of Turner and Constable have come to dominate the English School, yet surely Bonington, the brilliant but tragically short-lived master of his art, has his place among them, a valid and distinguished place.

CARLOS PEACOCK
LONDON, 1979

[1] Delacroix and Bonington worked together to introduce the English style of clothes and shoes to their young contemporaries in Paris. When Bonington visited England, we may safely assume that he took back with him not only artist's materials (in particular a kind of millboard with a smooth white surface, known at the time as 'Flemish ground') but also the latest in masculine fashions.

1. THE ROMANTIC MOVEMENT

IT sometimes seems that nations in their relationships to one another have, like men and women, their fleeting attachments, their marriages and estrangements, their divorces and reconciliations. And between ourselves and the French, what a diversity of feelings the centuries have brought, what strange intermixtures of hate and friendship, of admiration and contempt. But, curiously enough, it was after the long and bitter war with Napoleon that we and the French enjoyed a brief honeymoon of artistic rapprochement and also a degree of personal understanding unique in Anglo-French relations.[1]

After the Battle of Waterloo, the Duke of Wellington warned intending travellers to France not to make the journey, as the animosity against the British was so strong. Yet when one reads the letters and journals of those who did cross the Channel, one is constantly surprised at the lack of hostility they report, and one gets the impression that these undeterred travellers found life in France virtually unchanged and the French themselves anxious to forget old scores. After 1815, for a period of twenty years or so there existed between ourselves and the French a kind of intellectual and artistic partnership that brought us closer together perhaps than we have been at any time, before or since. It was as if for this brief spell the old barriers of incompatibility fell away and the twenty miles of dividing sea that had once been an isolating frontier became only a measure of propinquity. What caused this change of attitude, this discovery of England, as one might call it, by the French?

The explanation is that, at this particular moment in time, we, the British, had something of cultural importance to offer the French and indeed Europe as a whole: the Romantic movement. Like the Renaissance, it transformed philosophy and art by giving man a new image of himself. Individual feeling and perception were regarded as more valid than established forms and the social code. Man, according to the Romantic creed, was a free and independent spirit and, bound by no law but the individual conscience, derived his moral sense from his own feelings and sensations. This was how Rousseau had pictured him in those novels and treatises that had fascinated and scandalised Continental Europe in the eighteenth century. But the main effect of Rousseau's preaching was to rally the opposition and to make more rigid the social code that he had attacked.

In England there was no such revolutionary figure to inspire a fear of change and to create, as a reaction, a greater rigidity in art, politics and religion. Here, with our more flexible political system and the traditional freedom of our philosophical and religious thought, it was natural perhaps that the Romantic movement should be mainly an affair of taste and sensibility, rather than a revolutionary challenge to the established order. In its English form, it might be described as a particular climate of feeling that gradually evolved, giving individual expression and the imagination a new scope and freedom in every branch of art. Not only did this climate of feeling influence the way men wrote and painted, but it brought about the re-discovery of the Gothic style, and it produced, among other things, that peculiarly English art – landscape gardening, the taste for reshaping and beautifying the natural scene by human aid. It originated in the desire of eighteenth-century landowners to make the surroundings of their mansions more picturesque by the creation of vistas, the digging of ornamental lakes, the erection of classical temples and simulated ruins to dramatise a skyline or enhance a view. It marked the beginning of a new feeling for nature which was ultimately to play such a major part in the English Romantic movement.

Looking across the Channel in the early years of the nineteenth century, the French saw us as an artistically progressive nation possessing what they at this time lacked: a new philosophy of art and the freedom to express it. And what they particularly admired was the freshness of English landscape painting – its quality of observed naturalism that broke so completely with the tonal conventions of the past. We were fortunate perhaps in not having, as the French did, an inherited artistic tradition whose form and continuity were a matter of national pride, demanding of the artist endless repetitions of the accepted style. For the English landscape painters there were no such inhibiting conventions, and they had behind them the habit of direct observation which the art of water-colour had developed. For them the blank canvas or sketchbook page was the waiting medium for recording their immediate sensations and, in their response to nature, they were inspired by a sense of insight and discovery. It was this kind of free, direct painting by English artists which so impressed the French.

Any study of the relations between French and English art at the beginning of the nineteenth century must give the painter, Richard Parkes Bonington, a key place in this brief but fruitful partnership. English-born, but artistically an Anglo-French product, he created a kind of art that might be said to combine the French qualities of balance and tonal refinement with the naturalistic freedom of the English school. Less daring and diverse than Turner, less nature-orientated than Constable, he was influenced by them both, yet his art remained essentially his own and, in his landscapes, his richly detailed architectural subjects and, most of all, in his coast scenes and shipping pieces, he displayed individual qualities of style and feeling that place him in the forefront of the Romantic painters. But there is another side of his art which must not be forgotten – his figure studies and his paintings of subjects taken from history and literature. James Roberts, who knew Bonington in his student days, tells us:

'he always showed a strong liking for all sorts of historical traces. He loved to study the transitions from one style to another. He was fascinated by the works of Sir Walter

Head of a youth in 17th-century dress. Pencil. 1827.

Scott, especially those which had an archaelogical bent. I have no recollection of ever having seen Bonington interested in anything but questions of art or matters connected with it. With costumes, all from the Middle Ages onwards appealed to him. His excursions were all in accordance with his literary tastes. He had Barante's *History of the Dukes of Burgundy*, and, later, the memoirs which had furnished this author with the material for his works – books such as the chronicles of Enguerrand de Monstrelet and Froissart, whose archaic language had a particular charm for him. One often saw in his hands the early essays in French literature, such as those of Gerard de Nevers, Saintré, and Lancelot of the Lake, and also all the modern novels which had an archaeological flavour. He was, however, not so much dominated by a love of history

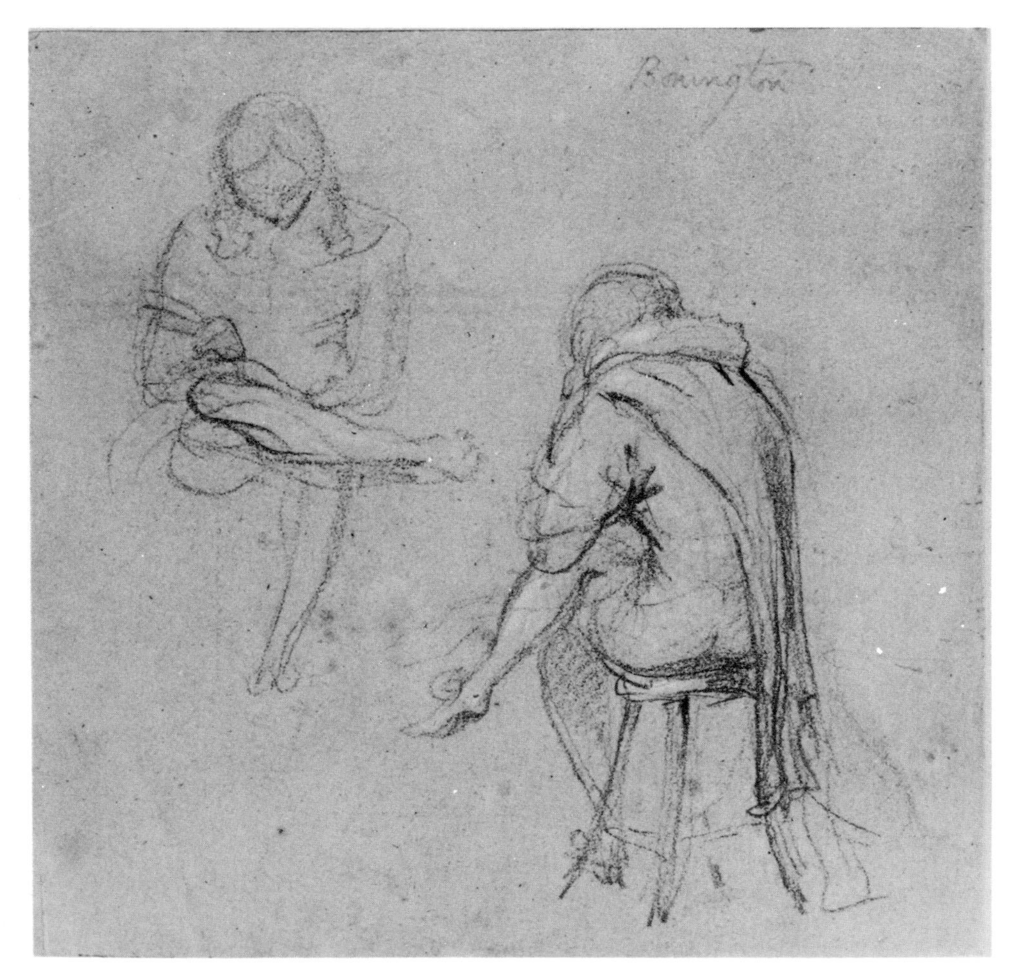

Study of two figures in 17th-century costume. Pencil heightened with white.

as fascinated by the sentiment which, in France, is called the historic colour sense – a sentiment characteristic among artists and strongly developed in him.'

To many of Bonington's contemporaries, the works inspired by literature and history were considered his greatest achievement, and if today we tend to regard them as his lesser works, they are a reminder that Bonington's art reflects every aspect of the Romantic creed: its love for the colourful and exotic, its taste for theatrical effect and its feeling for literature and the past. In these subject paintings and in those of his great French contemporary, Delacroix, one is constantly aware of the close relationship that existed then between painting and literature. The frequent borrowing of literary subjects by such painters as Bonington and Delacroix was perhaps an implicit recognition that their new freedom of expression, and the transformation of the artistic and philosophic climate which had created it, was largely due to the influence of the writer. And it was to the English writer especially that the Romantic movement owed its origin and development.

New movements come about in art when men see the world around them in a new way, thinking and feeling about it with a changed perception. Such movements are seldom sudden things, but tend to be the result of cumulative influences and the cross-fertilisation of one nation's art with another's. In the distant past it was the art of Italy which gave the Northern painters a basis and stimulus for their own innovations, as in the case of Dürer and Rembrandt. In the Romantic movement of the nineteenth century it was England that supplied the germinating influence, the essential philosophy that liberated art from the old restrictive forms. It was something that grew up slowly, and its beginnings might be traced back to the English novels of the eighteenth century, particularly those of Richardson, whose heroes and heroines initiated Europe into a new climate of sentiment and feeling. And again, in another field, English literature exerted a significant influence. It was largely through the novels of Sir Walter Scott that Europe acquired a new sense of history. In his writings he evoked the past in an imaginative way and he enriched the artistic consciousness of his own age by bringing it in touch with the life of other centuries. But this taste for history was something more than a contemporary fashion; it expressed perhaps a sense of the growing difference between the old world and the new, a realisation that the spread of scientific thought, the revolution in political and social ideas, the change in dress and manners, marked a new direction in human development. Looking back on the past, men saw it now in a new perspective, saw its art and colour with a fascination that reflected their feelings of difference. In calling this period 'romantic', we tend to forget that it was the first age of applied science and in it the modern consciousness might be said to have been born. But, at the beginning, art and science were in a kind of philosophic partnership, so that Constable (who seems to us essentially a painter of pre-scientific and rural England) could think of his landscape art as scientific painting, and regard his great scientific contemporary, Michael Faraday, as a fellow exponent of nature's truth.

In Bonington's art there is none of the Wordsworthian philosophy of nature which underlies Constable's. For Bonington the question of the relationship between art and science might have seemed an irrelevance but, curiously enough, it was scientific progress, in the form of mechanisation of the lace-making industry that started Bonington on his career as a painter.

Born after the close of the eighteenth century, he came upon the scene at a propitious moment when the way was open to him to exploit those qualities of freedom and spontaneity which were the essence of the new artistic creed. A true Romantic, he moved easily between the past and present and was fascinated by the power and brilliance of the Old Masters and the life of earlier centuries. Yet, in his own art, he was essentially 'modern', painting in a style that owed little to the past and which, in its most characteristic form, serves as a reminder that economy of effect and tonal refinement are not incompatible with Romantic self-expression.

If we regard the Romantic movement as mainly English in inspiration, we must take the English landscape painters, Constable, Bonington and Turner, as its representative figures, as the pioneer exponents of the new philosophy. Up until now English painting, with a few exceptions, had been very much a derivative and second-hand affair. Why, then, this sudden blossoming into originality? Perhaps 'sudden' is a misleading word as it belies the long seed growth out of which this blossoming came. But in the end, it seems, this transformation of English painting was hastened, perhaps even imposed, by the events of history.

The birth of the English water-colourists

Cut off from the rest of Europe by the Napoleonic wars, we were forced into an artistic self-sufficiency. Artists, therefore, had to content themselves with painting the English scene, which did not lend itself so readily to the classical conventions as did the more colourful and dramatic landscape of the Continent. Confined then to his native shores and, consequently, less prone to foreign influence, the English painter followed a path of his own, discovering that by personal observation and imaginative feeling he could transform the everyday aspects of nature into an art as valid and distinctive as anything in the past. And he was fortunate in having at hand a tradition that had already developed landscape painting into an essentially flexible and personal art – the tradition of water-colour.

Like the Romantic movement, the art of water-colour might be claimed as mainly an English invention, for it was the English artists of the nineteenth century – Bonington outstanding among them – who discovered for themselves the poetic qualities of the medium. Perhaps only one Continental artist, centuries before, had used water-colour in the same free and personal way: Dürer. One of the marks of great genius is that it anticipates in some way the sensibility and artistic forms of its successors and, when one studies the water-colours of Dürer, one cannot help being struck by their uncontemporary and 'romantic' quality. It seems that Dürer, in his intimate contacts with nature – in his studies of plants and animals, for example – or in his sketches of landscape under some particular sky or light, had found that only in the rapid, lucent medium of water-colour could he give a quality of life and freshness to what he saw.

Though at a far remove from Dürer, the nineteenth-century English artists used water-colour in much the same way, finding that this rapid and direct medium served them supremely well in the recording of observed effects. In fact, without the innovations and experiments in water-colour and without the habit of personal observation it encouraged, the oil painting of such artists as Turner and Constable would not have had the freedom and originality it so richly displays. For Bonington especially, water-colour was all-important from the first. It was his youthful training-ground and, later, when he worked in oils, he was still, in his mastery of delicate and luminous tones, a water-colourist at heart. Because this branch of art played such a major part in developing the poetic naturalism of English landscape painting, it is worth reminding ourselves of its origin, the advantage it possessed in being a flexible and adaptive medium, and in having no long history behind it to impose inhibiting conventions.

In England the systematic use of water-colour may be said to have begun in the days of the Grand Tour when rich eighteenth-century aristocrats took professional artists with them on their journeys through Europe. These artists were, in a sense, the cameramen of their day, for it was their function to record for their patrons the places and monuments they visited on their travels. Generally, of course, the focal point of these tours was Italy, and the artist, dutifully sketching the ruins of Pompeii or the Colosseum at Rome, soon discovered how adequately water-colour could meet the challenge of the Italian light and, in combination with pencil, could give to topographical accuracy the added charm of atmosphere and natural tone. In these quickly executed, on-the-spot drawings there were no pretensions to 'high art'. The artist recorded what he saw with little regard for rules and theory, and in meeting the need for topographical accuracy, he developed in many cases an art that was both stylistically new and distinctively his own. From these beginnings grew up the whole varied school of English water-colour; by exploring the possibilities of direct observation, the artists of this school influenced the philosophy of landscape painting as a whole. When one considers the work of certain important nineteenth-century artists, those equally at home in oils and water-colour, one has a sense of dual achievement, of a dichotomy in creative power. Among such English artists, Turner must take the first and foremost place, and Bonington, surely, the second.

[1] In the Middle Ages a rather similar kind of artistic partnership existed between ourselves and the French. In the twelfth century and in the thirteenth artists from Winchester and St Albans exerted a directive influence on French architecture, sculpture and painting. And later, English skill in the illuminating of manuscripts became so highly esteemed that English painters established themselves in Paris, helping to found the Parisian school which dominated northern Europe and even had some influence on Italian art. From France new developments in architecture and sculpture were brought to England, and it was from France that English stained-glass workers derived their models and designs.

2. THE EARLY LIFE OF BONINGTON

RICHARD PARKES BONINGTON was born at Arnold, Nottinghamshire, in 1802 and died in London in 1828, a month before his twenty-sixth birthday. With these dates in mind, one can only marvel at the prodigious productivity of his short creative life, the years from 1817 to 1828. He was one of those geniuses (and with certain reservations he could be classed as one) who reach maturity with only a minimum period of apprenticeship. In the world of poetry one finds a parallel in the brief life of Keats and, in music, in the tragically short careers of Schubert and Arriaga.

The life of Bonington is an example of those strange workings of chance which, like the shaking of a dice-box, somehow produce a supremely lucky throw. If Bonington's parents had not been worldly failures in their different ways, Bonington himself might never have set foot on the charmed path of international success. Yet, failures as these very ordinary parents were, each gave the painter something essential to his future. From his mother he had an educational background which must have quickened his interest in the literature of the past; from his feckless and ineffectual father he received a rudimentary grounding in the arts.

Soon after the painter's birth, Mrs Bonington opened a school at Arnold, just outside Nottingham, which, a few years later, when the prospects seemed propitious, she moved to larger premises in Nottingham itself. Her husband, who had begun life as the governor of Nottingham gaol but had been virtually dismissed for certain irregularities, became subsequently a dabbler in the arts. On the strength of having got a picture he had painted accepted by the Academy, he set himself up as a drawing master, teaching at the Nottingham Academy and at several schools in the county. He was also teacher of art in Mrs Bonington's school and he tried his hand as well as a seller of prints, writing paper, optical glasses, cameras oscuras and music. But this venture soon failed and within a year his entire stock was advertised for sale. A gossip-writer of the day gives us this account of the artist's father:

'Mr. Bonington had the reputation of being a good tavern companion, an open, generous-hearted man, but villainous company too often led him into unfortunate predicaments. One night, on returning home rather muddled, he was taken up for riotous and disorderly conduct – a rather awkward circumstance for the governor of the gaol, and one which nearly caused him his dismissal. It was not until the commission of a graver offence – such as conversing with prisoners on the subject of politics, and debating amongst them the question of free government and the reading to them the forbidden doctrines of Tom Paine – that, to adopt a modern phrase, he thought it fit to tender his resignation.'

Meanwhile, Mrs Bonington's school prospered steadily and the number of pupils grew. In 1809 she decided to take more commodious premises in Park Row, Nottingham. In the advertisement announcing this change she states with rhetorical pride:

'A situation more eligible could not have been chosen, as it combines every advantage of town and country. The premises are large and quite entire, with a convenient playground, the schoolroom 33 feet in length, and within a few paces of the Park.'

In these new and grander premises art was to have a major place. Mr Bonington

View of Calais jetty, and two views of the entrance to Calais harbour with Fort Rouge. Pencil. 1821-2.

announced that he was intending to open 'an exhibition room for portraits in oils etc. at his house in Park Row'.

Ryley, a contemporary actor, records a visit he paid to the Bonington household:

'A neat, accomplished female received me with much politeness and good humour. She was Mrs. Bonington. The whole of the dwelling impressed me with the respect of its owners, from the cleanliness and comfort visible in its arrangements. Mrs. Bonington indulged me with a view of her husband's work, at the same time conversing in a style superior to females in general.'

But in a few years the cloud of failure gathered over Mrs Bonington's scholastic venture as it had earlier done over her husband's business plans. The expenses of the house in Park Row became too heavy, and a move was made to humbler premises in Park Street. Here the school stagnated and declined, and after three years it was finally closed. What accounted for this failure we do not know for certain. It may be that parents wanted an educational establishment more stylish and imposing than the rather shabby Boningtons could provide. Or perhaps, as has been plausibly suggested, the failure of the school was due to the growth and commercialisation of the Nottingham lace industry, which drove the better families from the town. At all events, by 1817 the Boningtons were offering their services as visiting teachers:

'Mr. and Mrs. Bonington respectfully inform their friends and the public that their Drawing School will re-open on Monday 27th inst. They will also continue to attend schools and private families in Nottingham and its vicinity as usual.'

If it was the industrial inroads of the lace trade which had altered the social scene and robbed the Boningtons of their pupils, then it may have struck Mr Bonington that such changes could not be resisted and the wisest thing to do was to forget the unrewarding world of art and schools, and to seek success in the rising star of the new factory system. Whatever his reasoning, he decided to enter the lace trade himself and become a partner in the firm of Clarke, Webster and Bonington.

The plan behind this partnership was to set up a lace-making factory in Calais and then to capture the French market from inside. But the exporting of lace-making machinery was then illegal, so, for the plan to succeed, the machinery had to be surreptitiously shipped piece by piece and then re-assembled on the other side of the Channel. At the end of 1816, Clarke had got his loom set up in Calais, and the following year the Boningtons migrated from Nottingham to join him. It was with this move to France that the artistic career of young Bonington began.

Bonington's progress in France

We know from items that came up for sale after Bonington's death that he had shown an early talent with brush and pencil; and it seems that when the family migrated to Calais, Bonington's father expected his son to use his gifts for the designing of lace and to earn his keep by giving a hand in the actual manufacture of it. But, to a boy of fifteen possessed of a strong artistic urge and stimulated by new and picturesque surroundings, how dull and frustrating this lace-making business must have seemed. No wonder then that there were spells of truancy when young Bonington was lured away to sketch the colourful life of the port and the ancient buildings of the town. To the boy's father this neglect of the family business was inexcusable and he grew convinced that his son's taste for this unremunerative form of art was something to be checked. But if young Bonington ever made promises of reform, he seems to have broken them consistently, and when it came to the competing claims of lace and art, it was the art of the streets and quayside that was always the likely winner.

The influence of Louis Francia

It was during one of the sketching expeditions to the quays that Bonington made a chance encounter that was to shape the future pattern of his life. Here he met the professional artist Louis Francia; it was a meeting that was to have a decisive influence on the development of his art and, ultimately, to open the way to Paris and to those studies and contacts which were to transform him into the brilliant and original painter he so soon became.

As an artist, Louis Francia (1773-1839) might be called an Anglo-French hybrid, as Bonington himself might be. A native of Calais, Francia had crossed over to England to escape the French Revolution and had then established himself in London as a teacher of drawing. Here he became a follower of the English water-colour tradition and his contacts with Girtin led him to adopt a broad and powerful style that was essentially English in its feeling. After the restoration of the Bourbons in France, Francia returned to his native Calais, a disciple of the English water-colour school and an artist thoroughly grounded in its technique and in its naturalistic philosophy.

The momentous result of this meeting of Francia and Bonington on the quayside at Calais was that, for a few months, Francia became young Bonington's art master, teaching him the theory and practice of water-colour as he himself had learnt it during his *émigré* years in England, and, in particular, the clear, bold technique which had so impressed him in the work of Girtin. So by a curious turn of chance it

I *French river scene with fishing boats*. Water-colour. 1824.

II *Shipping off the coast of Kent*. Water-colour. 1825.

III *A boat beached in a port at low tide*. Oil. 1825.

IV *Landscape, sunset*. Water-colour. 1826.

Shore scene near Calais. Sepia wash. 1819.

was from a French master on French soil that this precocious English boy learnt a form of art which was then almost exclusively a product of his native country.

Under Francia's tuition young Bonington's art rapidly developed, showing a growing mastery in his shipping and landscape subjects. But the boy's father, who already had misgivings about his son's taste for art, now grew positively alarmed. If young Richard got carried away with these wild ideas, what would happen to the lace-designing, and to the future of the family business? Questions such as these must have come into old Bonington's head when he remembered what a dismal failure his own dabblings in art had been. He decided to take a firm stand. A strict ukase was issued to his son: no more art lessons, no more truancy from the factory and no more sketching.

Confident of his parental authority, old Bonington never seems to have doubted that the matter was settled and his orders were being implicitly obeyed. Perhaps to lull his father young Richard made a show of compliance and contrived some means of making his absences less noticeable. At all events, against parental orders, the sketching and the art lessons surreptitiously went on.

The Bonington legend does not tell us how the final crisis came, but at some unlucky moment the hoodwinked father discovered that he was being duped and that the banned lessons under Francia were still going on. In a tempestuous mood he hurried round to Francia's house to assert his parental authority and to demand that all art lessons cease immediately. Young Richard was hiding in an upstairs room while his father fumed and fretted down below. In the end Francia managed to get the irate father off the premises, a relief that provided at least a breathing space to devise some hasty plan. Francia realised that at this moment young Richard's artistic future hung in the balance and a now or never decision had to be made.

Francia had a patron named Morel who was a resident of Dunkirk and, after a hasty conference with Richard, Francia wrote him a letter of introduction to Morel which he urged him to present without delay. The die was cast. Without returning home, Richard set out with his introductory letter on the journey to Dunkirk.

We do not know how young Bonington travelled or who supplied the funds. But at Dunkirk Morel befriended him in a practical and sympathetic way. No doubt the letter from Francia explained the particular situation and assured Morel that he had a youth of exceptional promise on his hands. Probably, too, Bonington took specimens of his water-colours with him, which must have convinced Morel on the spot that Francia's high opinion was no partisan exaggeration.

A Breton lacemaker. Pencil.

3. BONINGTON'S DEVELOPMENT AS A PAINTER

AS FRANCIA had taken an inspired step in sending Bonington to Dunkirk, so Morel, in his turn, took one equally inspired: he sent Bonington on to Paris. It was a perceptive act on Morel's part. The provinces might supply subjects for a painter, but only a centre like Paris could give him the stimulus and training which would save him from seeing the world with narrow, provincial eyes. For an artist of Bonington's potentialities Paris was the obvious place and, by a stroke of luck or inspiration, Morel equipped him with a letter of introduction to a young painter who was then working there. This young man, unknown at this date, was destined to become the leading figure in the French Romantic movement and, in some respects perhaps, the father of modern art – Eugène Delacroix. Bonington never lived to see the status and prestige that Delacroix enjoyed in later years, yet even when he was still young and unknown all the incipient qualities were there: the Romantic sensibility, the acute intellect, and the powerful and inquiring mind.

It was probably in the spring of 1818 that Bonington arrived in Paris. Delacroix describes their first meeting in a letter written to Théophile Thoré Burger in 1861. But

Studies after Van Dyck. Water-colour. 1825.

Trees on a rocky bank. Pencil.

at that distance of time Delacroix falters in his dates, putting the meeting earlier than it actually was.

'When I met him for the first time I was very young myself and I was making studies in the Louvre gallery: it was about 1816 or 1817. I beheld a tall youth in a short jacket silently painting studies in water-colour, usually after Flemish landscapes. He was already astonishingly skilful in this genre, which at the time was an English novelty . . .'[1]

Thanks to Delacroix, we have this vivid glimpse of the youthful Bonington, a tall figure in a short jacket, making studies in water-colour from Flemish landscapes, overawed a little perhaps by his first contacts with the masterpieces of the past. But this copying in the Louvre was invaluable to him as a preliminary grounding for the two years of academic training that were later to complete what was, nominally, his artistic apprenticeship.

In May of 1818 Bonington's parents arrived in Paris and opened a lace-selling shop in the Rue des Tournelles. By now, it seems, young Richard's secret flight from Calais had been forgiven and, with the shop in the Rue des Tournelles to inspire new optimism in the Bonington household, the normal parental relationship appears to have been fully restored. But the question remains – what had Bonington lived on since his Calais days, where had he lodged? Had Francia or Morel's bounty kept him afloat until his parents moved to Paris? In Bonington's brief life documentary evidence is sparse at every stage. The year 1819, for instance, is virtually a blank and here, as so often, we have to fall back on supposition. But it can reasonably be assumed that he went on copying at the Louvre and that the facility in water-colour which Delacroix had noted was used for something more than copying. No doubt at this time Bonington did water-colours of his own – probably views of Paris which he sold for modest sums – so earning himself a few welcome francs. And he would have found the Paris of those days as fascinating to record as he had the quays and ancient buildings of Calais.

Writing of Paris as he remembered it a few years after Bonington's death, William Callow, the artist, gives us this description:

'. . . Paris was then as it had been for centuries. The streets were lighted by oil lanterns suspended down the middle by cords, were laid with cobble-stones with gutters down the centre, and without any side pavements; there was no sanitation, and whenever there was a storm the streets were flooded. The Tuileries were unfinished, and the

Studies of French military uniforms of the past. Pencil and water-colour. With the artist's colour notes in English and a French inscription at the bottom of the drawing 'Gardes Francaises Mousquetaire en 1610 Enseigne en 1580'. 1822.

whole of the Place du Carrousel was filled with houses, the stables of King Charles X, and bookstalls . . . In spite of these detriments, Paris, with its boulevards, was then more picturesque than it is at the present time.'[2]

It was this ancient, time-mellowed Paris that was painted with such luminous delicacy by Bonington, Callow, T. S. Boys and other artists who were followers of the Bonington tradition.

Bonington's apprenticeship with Gros

In 1820 Bonington began his formal artistic training by entering the atelier of Baron Gros in the École des Beaux Arts. Here he must have felt, as he would never have done in London, the fierce division between the old art and the new. In England a handful of collectors and connoisseurs might have argued the question in a series of papers, but in France the conflict between Classicism and Romanticism went much deeper. Classicism had become almost a patriotic symbol; it was seen as representing the old traditional France and, for this reason, it was officially fostered and encouraged. Napoleon, posing as the heir of Charlemagne and of the Holy Roman Empire, had identified himself with it for political reasons, believing that it served to give his new imperialism the ostensible stamp of the classical past. The art of Jacques-Louis David, with its strict adherence to classical principles, created to perfection the image and philosophy of this neo-classical France. But, with the fall of Napoleon and the gradual freeing of art from its official role, the old order was faced with the challenge of Romanticism – the new creed of artistic freedom, alien in origin and threatening the whole basis of the French tradition.

One can imagine the fierce arguments it must have caused among the students in Baron Gros' atelier, and for the majority, confronted as they inevitably were with the dreary routine of copying from classical casts, the new philosophy, with its emphasis on freedom and self-expression, must have seemed an exciting challenge to the academic preoccupation with the past. Even as a newcomer to the Baron's classes Bonington probably enjoyed a certain measure of prestige among his fellow students. For one thing, he came from England, the home of the new Romantic movement, and for another, his skill and originality in the use of water-colour must have soon impressed his companions in the atelier, as it later did Gros himself.

On the whole Bonington was fortunate in his teacher. Though Baron Gros had been a pupil of David and was, in principle, one of the old school, he was enough of an artist himself to be sensitive to change and to be able to offer help and

Etching made in 1847 by F. Villot from a sepia self-portrait by Bonington, originally in the possession of Baron Rivet. Original portrait 1823.

encouragement to the younger generation. On his side it is doubtful whether he found Bonington in any way a model pupil, but he discerned almost from the start the young man's particular kind of originality and his own inability to develop it by formal teaching.

There is a story that Gros came into the atelier one day, full of praise for some fresh and brilliant water-colours he had seen in the window of a shop. He advised his pupils to go and study these water-colours for themselves, though he could not say for certain who the artist was. The sequel to the story has two versions: one is that Bonington himself confessed to having done them, the other that some fellow student in the atelier told Gros that they were Bonington's work. Which version is the true one does not really matter. What is certainly fully corroborated is Gros' generous tribute to his young pupil on discovering that the water-colours he so much admired were by him. 'Oh,' said Gros, 'then why do you come here? You have nothing to learn and you are wasting your time.'

It speaks well for Gros, as a teacher and as a man of artistic perception, that he could show such unqualified appreciation of these water-colours by Bonington which had nothing of the grand style about them, and were in a medium that was at this time almost unknown in France. But Gros was not the only artist to be impressed. Delacroix also saw these water-colours in the art shop window, and in the letter to Thoré Burger already quoted he recalls them and describes the characteristic qualities which give Bonington's water-colours their special place:

'. . . At Schroth's newly opened gallery (the first of its kind, I fancy) where drawings and small pictures were for sale, I saw some water-colours which were delightful both in colour and composition. They already showed all the charm which is his special quality. To my mind, some other modern artists show qualities of strength or of accuracy in representation, which are superior to Bonington's, but nobody in this modern school, or possibly even before him, has had that lightness of touch which, particularly in water-colour, makes his pictures as it were like diamonds that delight the eye, quite independently of their subject or of any representational qualities.'

Théodore Géricault. *Three students studying a picture*. Water-colour. The figure on the far right is that of Bonington.

For two years, on and off, Bonington remained in Gros' atelier. The reason for his final departure in 1822 is uncertain. There are suggestions of a breach between master and pupil, but the most likely explanation is a realisation on both sides that, in this case, there was little to be gained from academic training. For Gros, one feels, Bonington must have been something of an enigma – this young English student deficient in so much of the art education that was judged to be essential by French

A woman sewing. Pencil. 1822-3.

Study of pack donkeys. Pencil. 1822-3.

Study of French peasants. Pencil. 1822-3.

classical standards, yet showing in his chosen medium a mastery of light and colour which gave him a distinction all his own.

If there is any truth in the suggestion that a personal rift developed between Gros and Bonington, one might hazard the guess that the cause of it was Bonington's expressed contempt for the lifeless and conventionalised art which David and his followers sought to impose upon the younger generation. What Bonington's feelings on this subject were can be judged from an account that James Roberts gives us of Bonington's reaction to a typical David work. On one occasion Roberts, who was a contemporary student in Gros' studio, went with Bonington to see David's *Rape of the Sabines*, the artist himself being present to exhibit his painting. In the foreground of this picture was the figure of a spearsman placed in such an unnatural attitude that no professional model could take the pose that the artist set him. In the end David explained with voluble pride that Madame Vestris, the famous dancer, had come to the rescue and had shown herself able and willing enough to oblige him by taking up this particular pose. 'These words', Roberts reports, 'brought to Bonington's face, which, I may say in parenthesis, was not very expressive, a pained look which passed away in a smile of pity and a shrug of the shoulders.'

While still enrolled among Gros' pupils, Bonington made a tour of the coast and towns of northern France. It is probably true to say that these towns and coastlines, the picturesque ports of northern France with their fisherfolk and shipping, counted for more in the creation of Bonington's art than all the formal instruction he received under Baron Gros. Sometimes a particular locality, by its personal associations or by some distinctive quality of its own, can exert a profound influence on an artist's style and become a recurrent inspiration in his work. For Cézanne it was the bare contours and dry, brickish tones of Provence; for Constable the pastoral scenery of the Stour Valley; for Bonington it was the cool blues and greys that characterise the chalky land of northern France. It was to this cool range of tones that his artistic sensibility responded from the start, and in his oils especially his basic method of painting was to place small, brilliant notes of colour against a large area of contrasting coolness.

It was probably after leaving Gros' studio in 1822 that Bonington began to experiment seriously in oils, but as a young artist needing a steady source of income, he was probably wise not to hurry into this new medium but rather to continue to concentrate his efforts on those brilliant water-colours which caught the eye so readily when displayed in art dealers' windows.

Two water-colours by him, *Vue prise à Lillebonne* and *Vue prise au Havre* were exhibited at the Paris Salon in 1822, a tribute to his skill in a medium he had used

Portrait of a French student. Oil. This portrait, which owes something to the French academic tradition, was probably painted while Bonington was studying under Baron Gros in Paris, 1820-22. The subject of this portrait may be Joseph Auguste Carrier (1800-78), who was a fellow student of Bonington in Gros' Paris atelier.

Fishing boats at Dunkirk. Water-colour.

with consummate ease ever since boyhood. In 1823 he visited Belgium and Flanders, deriving from his travels the subject for an oil painting exhibited at the Salon in the following year, *Étude de Flandre*.

For Bonington 1824 was a happy and prosperous year. Much of it was spent at Dunkirk with his friend and fellow student Alexandre Colin and, as he painted the familiar coast scenes, he must have felt a growing confidence in his artistic powers, a confidence justified by the work he exhibited at the Salon that year. Besides the *Étude de Flandre*, he exhibited three other oils and a water-colour, *Vue d'Abbeville*. At this Salon of 1824 it was Constable with his painting *The Haywain*[3] who was the dominant figure, and the conflicting opinions that his art aroused represent one of those turning points in the history of aésthetics. To what extent Constable influenced French art is still a debated question, but certainly his effect on Delacroix was considerable and, in this case, English artistic influence was reinforced by Delacroix's

A French fruit-seller. Pencil.

A woman crocheting. Pencil. 1822-3.

View near Quilleboeuf. Oil. 1823-4.

friendship with Bonington and the admiration he felt for the young painter's work.

Although Bonington attracted less attention at the Salon than Constable, he had every reason to feel that his own reputation was now firmly established. Indeed, he received official proof of it by being included among the artists who were awarded gold medals for the merit of their work. But this did not save him from being attacked by critics of the old school, who accused him of propagating a new and alien style, and of exerting a harmful influence on the younger generation of French painters who were associated with him.

The visit to England

In 1825 Bonington visited England in fulfilment of a plan made the previous year. We do not know the reason for this visit. It may be that he wanted to gauge the prospects of the art market here or to get a comprehensive estimate of the latest developments in English painting, something he could only do by studying them on the spot. Records of Bonington's movements on this visit are sparse, and there has been a temptation to fill in the gaps by guesswork or conjecture. But we know that he painted on the upper and lower reaches of the Thames, studied with Delacroix the armour in the Meyrick Collection, and in all probability had Delacroix as a sketching

Eugène Delacroix. *Sketches on the Thames, 1825*. Pencil heightened with white chalk on buff paper. Inscribed by the artist 'Londres Tamise'.

V *Near Boulogne*. Oil. 1826.

VI *Les salinières by Trouville*. Oil. 1826.

VII *River scene in France*. Oil. 1824-5.

VIII *Coast of Picardy*. Oil. 1823-4.

IX *Paris. Quai du Louvre.* Water-colour. 1828.

X *Boulogne sands.* Oil. 1827.

XI *Abbey of St Bertin, near St Omer*. Oil. 1823.

companion in Westminster Abbey and in Westminster Hall. We know, too, that he went to Hampton Court and was impressed there by Holbein's portrait of the Earl of Surrey. These are the only things we know with any reasonable degree of certainty about Bonington's visit to England in 1825.

On this occasion he had brought over with him from France a letter of introduction to Sir Thomas Lawrence, which for some reason he did not use. Perhaps he felt that at this stage of his career he might appear too much of a beginner and would only be received with a chilly condescension by the rich and fashionable Lawrence. Or it might be – and later evidence suggests that this was the case – that practical considerations rather than diffidence made Bonington decide not to use this letter then. Unlike his feckless father, he had an instinctive shrewdness in the management of his affairs, and he seems to have calculated that at this stage the wisest policy would be to keep this letter in reserve until his work was better known in England, when Lawrence's good opinion and influence might set the seal to his achievement.

Bonington had crossed over from France with his friend, the French artist Alexandre Colin, and in England he renewed contact with two artists he had previously known in Paris, Thales and Newton Fielding – brothers of the famous water-colourist, Copley Fielding. He also met the two French painters, Isabey and Enfantin, who were in England at this time. Among English artists with whom he became acquainted were Richard Westall, Samuel Prout and W. J. Cooke, the engraver. But the most lasting and fruitful artistic relationship that Bonington formed on this occasion was with Eugène Delacroix, whose first visit to England happened to coincide with Bonington's brief return to his native shores. The link between them, which had first been established when Bonington was copying in the Louvre, developed now into a close association, and, if for no other reason, this stay in England marked an important stage in Bonington's career, for it was on English soil that the two men formed a friendship that resulted for a time in the complete sharing of their artistic theories and ideals.

It is unfortunate that we know almost as little of Delacroix's movements in England at this time as we do of Bonington's. For some reason he ceased the writing of his journal in October 1824 and did not resume it again until his Moroccan journey in 1832. So for a record of his three months' stay in England we have only the few surviving letters which Delacroix wrote to his friends in France. In one of these letters, dated 1 August, 1825, he says:

'I am crazy about sailing and I may shortly go down to Cornwall with Eugène Isabey who is here and who's a very good fellow. This would be a fortnight's voyage along the wildest coast of England, which might prove profitable enough in the long run to make up for any expenses I might incur at the time.'

A mention of Delacroix's proposed sailing expedition is relevant here because there is a legendary suggestion that Bonington accompanied him on this Cornish voyage. Certainly Cornish subjects have appeared in sale-rooms under Bonington's name, and there is an engraving of a Bonington painting with the title *Sea-shore, Cornwall*; but in this picture the coast formation suggests the cliffs of northern France rather than those of Cornwall, and the figures on the beach have a distinctly French look. On the whole, then, the possibility that Bonington and Delacroix were together on this Cornish trip is a remote one, though it cannot be completely ruled out.

Bonington's return to France

On his return to France Bonington shared Delacroix's studio in Paris for a time. This working partnership, temporary though it was, had significant advantages for both men. For Delacroix it provided the stimulus of Bonington's company and the inspiring enthusiasm which a young painter of Bonington's kind invariably communicates as he explores the scope and possibilities of his art. For Bonington there was the benefit of Delacroix's intellectual grasp, and the knowledge and insight with which he studied the art of earlier centuries. An American critic once described Delacroix as 'museum bred', meaning it in a derogatory sense. But this surely misses the point. Delacroix's interest in the past was not narrowly academic; he used it creatively and absorbed into his own art the richness and fluency of Rubens, the shadowy depths of Rembrandt and the brilliant colouring of the great Venetian masters. But he did it in a free and imaginative way that makes him not an academic copyist, but a pioneer figure in modern art.

Writing to his friend, Charles Soulier, from Paris in January, 1826, Delacroix speaks of the benefit he has derived from having Bonington as a studio companion:

'I had Bonington with me in my studio for some time. I was very sorry you weren't there. There's a tremendous deal to be gained from the company of that jolly fellow *(ce luron-là)* and I swear I am all the better for it.'

After leaving Delacroix's studio, Bonington took a large painting-room which he shared with the English artist, Frederick Tayler. Probably, with his growing output, he felt the need for extra space, and he may have been prompted too by a fear that in

Stage-coach passengers. Pencil. 1825.

A Normandy farmhouse. Pencil.

working at close quarters with Delacroix he was in danger of absorbing too much of the Frenchman's style and manner into his own art. Yet it was under Delacroix's influence that he had found themes for his art in the romance and colour of the East, and in those subjects from literature and history which were to become the stock material for so many lesser painters throughout the nineteenth century.

Frederick Tayler must be classed among these lesser artists, though in his day he was an eminently successful one. He became President of the Royal Watercolour Society in 1858 and received numerous foreign decorations and awards in the course of a long lifetime. His most characteristic works are sporting subjects, illustrations of past times, and, in particular, hunting and hawking scenes where the past is colourfully evoked by the use of seventeenth-century costume.

He and Bonington, it seems, met in a Calais hotel when Bonington was on his way back from England. As the result of a quickly formed friendship – they were the same age – they agreed to take a studio together in Paris. Tayler was a pupil of Horace Vernet, and it was probably at Tayler's suggestion that Bonington finally took the large painting-room in Paris which Vernet had used for his study of horses. Tayler recounted an incident that occurred in this studio while Bonington was away and he himself was engaged in painting a commissioned picture of a horse:

Henri Monnier. *Bonington in his studio.* Pencil and sepia wash.

'I was painting a portrait of a horse for Lord Henry Seymour when suddenly the French cook entered the room, bearing a set of *couverts* on his head. This so frightened the horse that he broke from the lad who held him and dashed at full speed round the room, kicking out in all directions, to the great danger of Bonington's pictures, which were placed on the ground. A favourite pointer dog of mine left the room, also at full speed, and I could never hear any tidings of it afterwards. Soon after this Bonington returned from Rome.'

After his visit to England in 1825, Bonington seems to have become convinced that his steadiest and most lucrative market was in his native country, and from then on he took every opportunity of getting his work known across the Channel. In January 1826 he exhibited two paintings at the British Institution, *French coast scenery* and *French coast with fishermen*. Both were sold and were given rapturous notices by the *Literary Gazette*.

The critic asked:

'Who is R. P. Bonington? We never saw *his name* in any catalogue before, and yet here are pictures which would grace the foremost *name* in landscape art. Sunshine,

River scene, with fishermen in a punt. Water-colour.

perspective, vigour, a fine sense of beauty in disposing of colours, whether in masses or in mere bits – these are extraordinary ornaments to the rooms.'

Again, two weeks later, the same critic, referring to the *French coast with fishermen*, writes:

'Few pictures have more skilfully expressed the character of open sunny daylight than

Portrait of Lord Henry Seymour in a riding cap. Oil on panel. *c.* 1827.

Fish market, Boulogne. Oil.

the one under notice, and we have seldom seen an artist make more of the simple materials which the subject afforded. With a broad unfinished pencil, he has preserved the character of his figures and accessories; also a splendid tone of colour, glowing and transparent.'

It is clear from these notices that Bonington's name was virtually unknown in England at the time and that his work, with its individual style and technical

Man lying on a settee, reading. Pencil and water-colour. Inscribed by the artist on lower edge of drawing 'Companion de voyage'. Bonington seems to have forgotten that the French spelling here should be *compagnon*. 1826.

assurance, came as a revelation to the English public. In Paris, on the other hand, Bonington was by then an established figure, had shared its artistic life ever since his student days, and was generally known as one of the leaders of the new school. Through Delacroix he had been brought into contact with eminent intellectuals and with wealthy patrons of the arts and, as his fame increased, the circle of his friends became more numerous and influential.

The trip to Italy

It was in company with Baron Charles Rivet, friend of Delacroix and wealthy patron of the new Romantic School, and himself an artist, that Bonington went to Venice in the spring of 1826. Starting from Paris on 4 April, they were away on their travels for eleven weeks. During this time Rivet kept a diary which is the only document we have which gives us any day to day account of Bonington's activities. From Paris the route southward took the two travellers through Semur and Dole, and then on to Geneva, where they stayed for a while before crossing the Alps by way of Sion and Brig. On arriving in Italy, they lingered for a few days in Milan, then moved on through Brescia to Verona, which they reached on 18 April. Two days later they arrived in Venice.

Dull, overcast weather had made the journey an uninspiring one for Bonington. And, in Venice, rain and leaden skies disappointed his expectations. Venice in sunlight has become so much an artistic convention that one is tempted sometimes to regret that Bonington did not paint it as he first saw it, a city of weeping skies and

A woman at prayer. Pencil.

Venice from the Lido. Pencil heightened with white on blue paper. Inscribed 'Vue prise du Lido'. 1826.

grey lagoons. In comparison with Turner and Constable Bonington may seem limited in his atmospheric range, but for him a particular quality of clear, diffused sunlight, rather than varied atmospheric effects or the drama of the rain cloud, was almost a prerequisite element in his landscape art. In Venice, under clouded skies, this lover of clear sunlit tones sank, Rivet noted, into a dismal mood.

Then, at last, the weather cleared and Bonington's drooping spirits rose. Venice dazzled him with its architecture and its expanse of water, and by the brilliant costumes of the past which glowed out from the paintings by the great Venetian masters. For Romantic painters like Bonington and Delacroix there was a fascination in the costumes of earlier centuries, particularly those of the Renaissance with their rich textures and ornate accessories. Here, among this fabulous profusion of paintings and monuments, Bonington must have found all the colour and artistry he ever dreamed of.

Venice from the Lagoon. Oil. 1826.

This visit to Venice undoubtedly helped to develop his historical sense and it inspired him to emulate in his own figure subjects the glowing colours of the early Venetian painters. But his immediate impressions of the city are recorded in a masterly series of water-colours and pencil drawings, sketches of the architecture, the lagoons, the shipping – all done with the quality of poetical precision which

Venice. Study of the Colleoni Monument. Pencil. 1826.

Verona. Piazza dell'Erbe. Pencil heightened with white. 1826.

Venice. The Doge's Palace. Pencil. 1826.

Bonington achieves so effortlessly in his water-colours and pencil studies.

If Venice was slow in revealing the enchantment of her light and sun, she did so ultimately with a power that Bonington found irresistible. When on 20 May, after three weeks, it was time to wrench himself away, he grieved at the loss, and Rivet noted in his diary the silence that fell on him when they left the lagoons. Travelling back from Venice, they passed through Padua, Ferrara and Bologna; and, on reaching Florence, spent a week there which enabled them to visit Pisa. Then continuing their journey, they went through Sarzana, Lerici, La Spezia, Genoa, Alessandria and Turin.

When Bonington finally returned to Paris on 20 June, he must have been delighted at the way his affairs had prospered in his absence and at the dazzling promise of success which the future seemed to hold. When in Venice, he had received a letter from his father telling him that all the paintings done in the first half of the year had been sold, and now, on his return to Paris, he found the money waiting for him. The sum earned since January, Rivet records, was between 7,000 and 8,000 francs. Besides these tangible gains he had the Italian experience behind him as well as a whole new range of subjects which an artist of his gifts could use to marvellous advantage.

Genoa. Pencil on grey paper. Inscribed 'Genoa'. 1826.

XII *The Doge's Palace, Venice*. Water-colour. 1827.

XIII *Lake Lugano*. Oil. 1826.

XIV *Piazza San Marco, Venice.*
Water-colour. 1827.

XV *Venice. The Grand Canal*. Oil. 1827.

XVI *Verona. Corso Sant'Anastasia.*
Water-colour. 1826.

Verona. Tomb of Mastino II. Pencil.
1826.

Thomas Shotter Boys. *Interior of Bonington's studio, Paris.* Pen and bistre ink. Inscribed at lower left of drawing 'Bonington's atelier, Paris. Rue des Martyrs, no. 11'.

[1] This and subsequent quotations are from *Eugène Delacroix: Selected Letters*, edited and translated by Jean Stewart (Eyre & Spottiswoode), 1971.
[2] William Callow, *Autobiography* (A. & C. Black), 1908.
[3] When first exhibited at the Royal Academy in 1821, it was seen by the French painter, Théodore Géricault, who was in London at the time. Another Frenchman, Charles Nodier, also saw it and mentioned it glowingly in a book of his experiences: *Promenade de Dieppe aux Montagnes d'Écosse.*

4. BONINGTON'S LAST YEARS

BUT over the glowing vista of the future an ominous shadow had already fallen. Rivet had noticed on the Italian journey a diminution in Bonington's strength and by the following year a definite weakness had set in. Perhaps the Italian journey, with its arduous travelling and its slavish pressure of work, had undermined his constitution, making it vulnerable to the onset of tuberculosis. Though the year 1827 was marked for Bonington by a state of growing weakness, he still worked with feverish energy. It was as if he felt that he must devote every moment to his art while enough of his strength remained. There was much to do. He was pressed with many commissions from collectors, and there were the Italian sketches to be worked up into exhibition

Swiss girls at Meyringen. Pencil. 1826.

Venice. Church of San Giorgio dei Greci.
Inscribed in the artist's hand 'Eglise des Grecs, Venice'. Pencil. 1826.

pictures. He was also planning to make historical and literary subjects a major feature of his art.

In spite of failing health, he took steps that year, as he had done previously, to safeguard his professional income; to ensure, by developing his English contacts, that he was not over-dependent on the French market. In practical affairs this young Romantic painter showed qualities of foresight and prudence which seem as much part of his nature as his inspired facility in art. Living in Paris, he was in a position to judge for himself the instability of French political life, and his characteristic reaction was to take practical measures to guard against the financial depression that any social upheaval would inevitably bring.

As we have seen, the visit to England in 1825 was to some extent the first stage in his search for an international market, and in the succeeding months the conviction seems to have grown on him that a hedge against a drop in French picture buying was more than ever necessary. Already there were warning signs; in 1826 the art dealer Schroth was forced by financial difficulties to curtail his buying of oil paintings, reverting finally to his original trade of print-selling. Schroth had been an important link in Anglo-French art. He had helped at the beginning of Bonington's career to bring his work before the public and he was one of the French dealers who had come over to London to buy paintings from Constable for the Paris connoisseurs. This contraction of his business was therefore a serious blow to the Modern school. And there were other dealers who had handled the work of contemporary artists and who now found themselves financially in even deeper water – Arrowsmith, for instance, the Parisian dealer of English origin who, like Schroth, had been a regular buyer of Constable's work in London until impending bankruptcy ended the connection.[1]

Schroth's decline must have warned Bonington that the time had come to make London, rather than Paris, the main outlet for his work. And, as a first step towards keeping his name before the English public, it was necessary to become a regular exhibitor at the Royal Academy and the British Institution; he would need, too, some influential figure in the London art world to act as his agent, to arrange sales and commissions among that new circle of English connoisseurs who were already eager buyers of his work. And what better agent than the London dealer, Dominic Colnaghi,[2] who by family tradition and his own taste and knowledge had acquired an unquestioned prestige in all matters of art?

In 1827 Bonington exhibited for the first time at the Royal Academy in London, and in the summer of that year he came again to England, probably with the express purpose of making contact with Colnaghi. As a result, it seems, commissions from

my Dear Friend

From your questions about the size of the picture I am about for Mr Carpenter and your silence respecting the pictures Mrs Carpenter wished to exibit here, I fear you have not received my letter in answer to yours principally regarding Mrs C's wish to exibit [illegible] should it so have happened you must have taxed me with a most rude indifference & neglect — on the contrary I should feel most happy in being the means of placing any of Mrs C's works in our exibition — respecting which I will repeat a few particulars of my last — the exibition will open on the 4th of Novbre and will continue so for 3 or 4 months — at the end of each month the 3 paintings an artist has the right to exibit may be changed for 3 other, so that should Mrs C still wish to send, the paintings will yet arrive in time for the first or second renewal, in such case

direct them to Mr Lagache Hotel [illegible] à Calais to be forwarded to me at Paris — in case frames are wanted write as soon as possible with the size — [illegible] above [illegible] contained divers happy conceits, marvellously [illegible], passing pretty, as well as of [illegible] morality [illegible] looking over your waggon load of items and [illegible] my large picture is some 3 feet by four a View of Venice somewhat thus — [illegible] I hope to get a few drawings done very soon — for my large picture I have promised the refusal of it to a person a friend of his, who was over here lately, for fear there is but little [illegible] chance, so the matter stands — the price I mentioned was 125 guineas, I hope to send it over for this winters exibition in Pall Mall and should you be able to put the question [illegible] till then, perhaps it may still be lucky enough to please Mr C — "somewhat too much of this" but I fear that I must end here for my wit is not over plentiful & I have none ready made for the present must

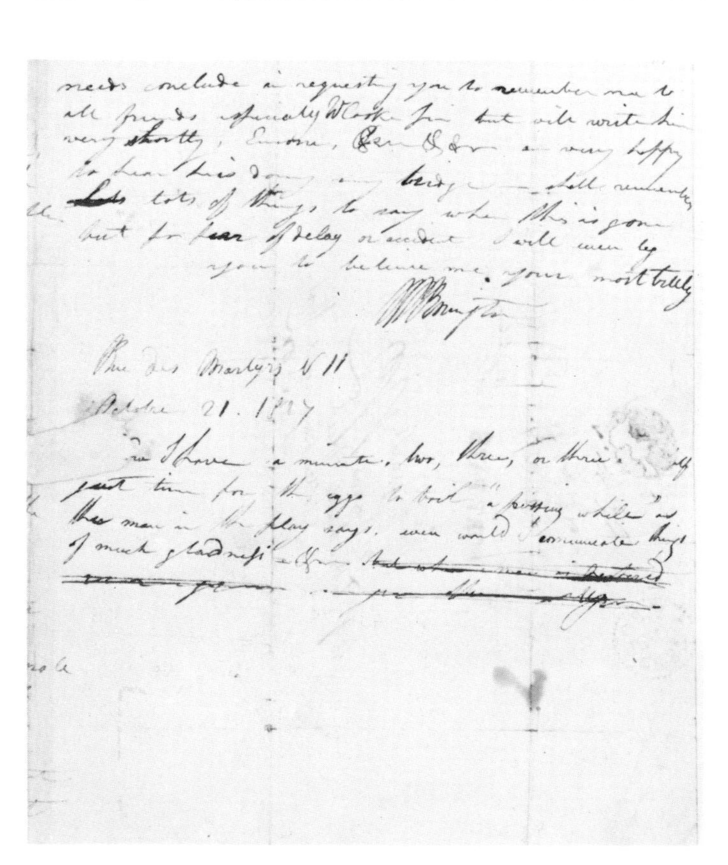

needs conclude in requesting you to remember me to all friends especially [illegible] but will write him very shortly, [illegible] am very happy to hear he is doing [illegible] still remember lots of things to say when this is gone but for fear of delay or accident I will even beg you to believe me your most truly

R P Bonington

Rue des Martyrs N 11

Octobre 21. 1827

[illegible] I have a minute, two, three, or three [illegible] just time for the eggs to boil a pretty while as the man in the play says, even would I communicate things of much gladness [illegible]

Letter from Bonington to his friend John Barnett of London, addressed from 11 Rue des Martyrs, Paris, and dated *Octobre* 21, 1827. The pen drawing in this letter relates to an oil sketch of Venice now in the National Gallery of Scotland. The finished version of this subject is in a private collection.

Colnaghi were arranged, and Bonington's friend and patron, John Barnett of Tottenham Street, London, also commissioned works from him and was eager with suggestions for future projects. Among Bonington's other friends in England were the members of the Cooke family, distinguished in the field of art and engraving, and the Carpenters, father and son, who were sellers of books and prints in Bond Street. Though Bonington and Constable apparently never met, the Carpenters provided a

Fisherfolk on the Normandy coast. Oil. 1827.

kind of artistic link between them. The father, James Carpenter, had been an early admirer of Constable's work and had bought a lock scene by him in 1814, a painting which Bonington must have seen, together, perhaps, with other works by Constable, in the Carpenters' home. The sale of this lock scene had given Constable particular satisfaction at the time because Carpenter was then a complete stranger to him and had bought the painting only because he liked it. Subsequently, Constable bought or borrowed books from the Carpenters or asked them to provide him with biographical details of painters from the art books in their stock. After Bonington's death, Constable wrote to young William Carpenter, asking him for 'a print or two of Bonington's', though in this letter he is critical of the dead artist's qualities of dash and finish, alleging that they came too easily and that they were superficially acquired without the disciplinary pains and study which a moral feeling in art imposes on a painter.

Though Bonington must have been on terms of close friendship with the Carpenters, they have left us no verbal record of the relationship; but William's wife, Margaret, a professional artist of some skill and sensitivity, did one or two sketches of him, as well as the posthumous portrait in oils which now hangs in the National Portrait Gallery, London.

Bonington returned to Paris with new commitments on his hands, as though in defiance of his failing strength. At the Paris Salon of November he exhibited *Vue du Palais Ducal à Venise*, *Vue de la Cathédrale de Rouen* and an impressive water-colour of St Omer. Three months later, in the second supplement of exhibits, these works were changed for three more: *Francis I et Marguerite de Navarre* (now in the Wallace Collection, London), *Vue de l'Entrée du Canal à Venise*, and a water-colour of an unspecified subject. At the British Institution he exhibited two Venetian scenes, *View of the Piazetta* and *The Ducal Palace* (both now in the Tate Gallery, London).

Return to England

In the spring of 1828 Bonington was in London again, possibly to arrange his works for the Royal Academy exhibition that was to open in May. It is curious that records of his movements in his last years are, with the exception of Rivet's diary, as scanty as those of his student days. But it appears that on this visit to England he at last used the letter of introduction to Sir Thomas Lawrence, given him by Mrs Forster, wife of the British chaplain in Paris, and that he took this opportunity of showing Lawrence some examples of his work. As Lawrence was a portrait painter, we can assume that the works that Bonington showed him were figure subjects, rather than coast scenes or

Man on a settee reading a newspaper.
Pencil. 1828.

landscapes. In this case it may well be, as Dr Marion Spencer has suggested, that the painting *Henry III and the English Ambassador* (now in the Wallace Collection, London) was among the works submitted to Lawrence for his judgement. If so, the choice was a judicious one, for Bonington has posed his figures here with a quality of theatrical elegance that must have appealed to a portrait painter who understood so well how a touch of the dramatic could flatter the human form. And, at this point, we may ask ourselves again why Bonington had so long postponed his meeting with Lawrence, why had he kept Mrs Forster's letter of introduction until this particular occasion? Was it youthful diffidence, a shrewd sense of timing, or did Mrs Forster herself have finally to prompt Bonington to make the move?

Whatever the reason, Bonington must have felt that nothing had been lost by the delay. At an age when most artists are still only hopeful aspirants he had achieved outstanding success in Paris and London, and an aura of celebrity was beginning to gather round his name. If he still had any doubts about his powers, there were critics enough in both capitals to flatter and reassure him. With all these tokens of success behind him there was surely no need to feel hesitant now in making himself known to the formidable, but courtly, Lawrence.

At the Academy in May Bonington exhibited two works, *Grand Canal with the Church of the Vergine della Salute*, and *Henry III of France*. Writing of these exhibits, the critic of the *Literary Gazette* says of Bonington:

'In a very short period this able artist has so distinguished himself by the brilliant character of his pencil, that his name to any piece is a sufficient guarantee of its excellence.'

But the sustained efforts of these final months, the strain and pressure of the unremitting work that Bonington had set himself, proved disastrous. When he returned to Paris, he sank into a state of weakness and exhaustion. Yet the creative urge in him was undiminished, and he believed that a sketching tour of Normandy would help to restore him. In making plans for this Nomrandy tour he arranged for his friend and fellow-painter, Huet, to join him there, but before he could start his health suddenly worsened and he was unable to leave Paris. Now he was so incapacitated that it was only with the help of friends that he managed to reach the Bois de Boulogne for a change of air and scene. By midsummer of 1828 he had regressed to such an extent that an invalid chair was necessary. The final crisis in his health came about through sunstroke, incurred while he was sketching on the banks of the Seine.

As a last, desperate resort, it was decided that the Bonington family should move to England where the fast-sinking Richard could put himself in the hands of a London doctor who had acquired notoriety at the time by his spurious claims for the successful treatment of rheumatism and tuberculosis. The journey from Paris was made in stages, the family arriving at Abbeville on 6 September. By now Bonington was so weak that he was only able to sign his name to a letter he dictated to his mother for John Barnett, explaining that he had become so ill that he was travelling to England to seek medical advice. In a postscript to this letter Mrs Bonington expressed her own feelings of despair.

On his arrival in London Bonington stayed with John Barnett at 29 Tottenham Street. Though a dying man, his work was still in the forefront of his mind and he seems never to have lost his interest in artistic experiment and innovation. Towards the end he was taken to see his engraver, W. J. Cooke, and on this occasion, supported on chairs, he made sketches in a new brown ink that Cooke was then testing. A description of the scene is given us by John Saddler, an engraver who was at this time serving his apprenticeship with Cooke.

Saddler writes:

'I was a pupil of William John Cooke, the engraver, and close friend of Bonington, and had been a month with him when Bonington came to dinner. I have some curious reminiscences of the day. It happened that my master was, at the instigation of his brother-in-law, Thomas Shotter Boys, making experiments for a permanent brown ink over which colour could be washed. One of the materials was walnut juice extracted from the outside shells and boiled down to expel the watery particles – and Bonington after dinner, while reclining on two or three chairs, made sundry sketches, with pencil and brush with the juice, and expressed his intention when he was better he should try the material further, adding his approbation of the colour – permanency had not been tried. They were brought into the study to be thrown in the paper basket, but I took care of them, with Mr Cooke's permission, and I have them now . . . They are simply curious (the ink sketches) as the very last things Bonington produced – he died after that visit.'

It is a touching glimpse that Saddler gives us of the young artist reduced to such physical weakness that he needed to be propped on chairs while he worked with brush and pencil, but still optimistic enough to speak of giving the walnut juice medium a fuller trial when his health improved. But that day was never to come. He died on 23 September 1828, a month before his twenty-sixth birthday.

Bonington died at John Barnett's house and was buried at St James's Church, Pentonville.[3] At his funeral a number of Royal Academicians followed the cortège led by Sir Thomas Lawrence, their President.[4] This official tribute to a painter who had not yet reached the age of twenty-six shows what a unique place Bonington had gained among the artists of the day. What kind of person was this young and brilliantly successful painter? Here, as in so much else relating to Bonington, the evidence is scanty, but what there is suggests a character essentially modest, a person tending to silence in company, but lively and communicative with those who overcame his natural reserve. But there was also, it seems, a gregarious side of him.

There are sketches by Bonington of artists' feasts and revellings which suggest by their vivid, first-hand quality that the painter of them could enjoy mixing in wild and boisterous company. Such scenes probably took place in the rambling old yellow house known as 'Childeberte', near the Place St Germain-des-Prés, a dirty, dilapidated warren which had housed artists for over forty years and which Bonington used to frequent in the company of Mademoiselle Rose, the model and mistress whom he and Delacroix shared.[5]

In his early days in Paris Bonington's charm of personality created friendships and sympathies which helped to lessen his inevitable sense of isolation. There was, for instance, his relationship with Madame Hulin, who owned a shop for the sale of artists' materials and pictures, and who was an important figure in the artistic life of Paris. It is said that she developed an affection for the young English artist and assisted him by showing his water-colours in her window and promoting their sale among her many influential patrons. And again, in the case of Baron Gros, it must have been some personal quality in Bonington that made him tolerate a pupil who was lax and wayward in his work, who saw no virtue in drawing from classical casts, and who was openly inclined to question the whole basis of the Baron's teaching.

Though we may reject the claim that Bonington was French by adoption, we can understand how easy it was for the French to refer to him as '*notre*' Bonington, as they did in their obituary notices. After all, it was in France that his artistic gifts first developed and it was in France that virtually the whole of his brief working life was spent. The dual nature of his roots – the Anglo-French mixture in him – comes out amusingly in a bilingual note sent by him to his friend and follower, Thomas Shotter Boys. In this note,[6] probably written shortly after Bonington's return from Italy in 1826, Boys is urged to come round to Bonington's studio at 11 Rue des Martyrs, Paris, where Monsieur Auguste, the orientalist and friend of Delacroix and Bonington, is to be the guest of honour. In this playful mixture of French and English (I have added the punctuation which the writer, in his haste, omitted) we glimpse for a moment the light-hearted side of Bonington.

'Dear Boys,
'Try and come this evening. Rivet and a few friends will be here, avec the french model and tout cela pour réjouir le chrétien. M. Auguste à qui appartiennent les honneurs de la soirée ne sera pas moins aise de vous voir que

'votre ami,
'Bonington'

'ce Mardi Matin'

When we consider the part France played in Bonington's history, we have to concede that it is almost entirely from French sources and, in particular from his fellow artists across the Channel, that our knowledge of Bonington comes. There was, for instance, no English artist who worked with him and could tell us with the authority of personal contact, as the French painter Paul Huet does, that Bonington had '*le genie de l'aperçu . . . un aperçu fin et juste de la nature*'. With Alexandre Colin, his closest friend among the younger French painters, Bonington kept up a correspondence which some misguided hand subsequently destroyed.[7] Only a few fragments survive, but in one there is a description by Bonington of a storm, and the feelings it evoked in him. One can almost catch the note of excitement in the terse and hurried way he reports the experience to Colin:

'a splendid storm since you left. I saw it from the end of the enclosure: I heard everything. My friend, it was superb! I was simply soaked.'

Portrait of Miss Montague Cook as a child. Pencil. 1825.

Bonington's approach to his art

Bonington's enjoyment of the storm reflects the fascination that such moments had for the Romantic sensibility of the time. In this respect Bonington was very much a product of his age, a painter schooled in the new philosophy that made personal feeling the key factor in life and art. Yet, unlike some of his English contemporaries, he never pursued sensation for its own sake, never became addicted to it in its extreme and violent forms. Delacroix, with his more complex psychology, seems to have had moments in his life when he needed themes of death and violence to spur on his creative powers. And, in the case of Géricault, there was a tendency to satisfy some sadistic side of his nature by the choice of brutal and violent subjects.

But with Bonington there were no such complications. The darker world in which Géricault and Delacroix tended to move was alien to him and he never sought to inject drama and sensation into his work by painting subjects that would pain or shock. It was, perhaps, his direct, uncomplicated nature that attracted Delacroix to him, a boyish zest that made a stimulating contrast to Delacroix's more introvertive personality. For Delacroix there was always a danger that the intellectual side of him might take control, causing his art to seem contrived and laboured. Bonington, on the other hand, the lyric painter, guided by feeling and instinct rather than the intellect, was inclined to paint with a kind of improvisatory freedom, sometimes losing his way in the process and being forced to abandon the picture he had started. But his zest and facility were so great that he would begin another immediately, succeeding here with the sustained inspiration that had eluded him at the first attempt. Delacroix said of his dexterity, '*Cette main était si habile qu'elle devançait la pensée.*' When he speaks here of Bonington's hand being so skilled that it ran ahead of his ideas, he refers to Bonington's gift of technical mastery which put him in that rare class of painters who seem to have come into the world fully equipped – the artistic prodigies, the *talents faciles.*

It is fortunate for us that the impression he made on Delacroix was such a deep and lasting one, surviving through Delacroix's long and eventful life, to be recalled for Thoré years afterwards with a vividness that eloquently testifies to the special place that Bonington retained in Delacroix's mind. 'I knew him well, and I was very fond of him,' Delacroix tells Thoré. 'Despite his imperturbable British sang-froid, he lacked

Port scene, with sailing vessels and shore buildings in the distance. Water-colour.

none of the qualities that make life enjoyable.'

So Delacroix writes of Bonington over forty years after first encountering him in the gallery of the Louvre, the tall English youth making studies in water-colour of the paintings there. But Bonington's legacy to Delacroix was more than the memory of a happy and stimulating friendship. Through this contact with Bonington a branch of Delacroix's art was developed in a way that it might not otherwise have been – his use of water-colour. Without Bonington's example and also, we may reasonably assume, without his practical instruction, Delacroix's water-colours might never have been the

Seascape with sailing vessels. Sepia wash.

XVII *A cutter and other shipping in a breeze*. Water-colour. 1827.

XVIII *Parterre d'eau à Versailles*. Oil. 1826.

XIX *Henri III and the English Ambassador*. Oil. 1827-8.

XX *The undercliff*. Water-colour. Inscribed on the back of the drawing in Mrs Bonington's hand, 'August 6 & 7th. 1828. The last drawing made by our dear son about prior to his fatal dissolution. Never to be parted with. E. Bonington.' 1828.

Near Burnham, Berkshire. Water-colour. 1828.

wonderful things they undoubtedly are.

The personal quality of Bonington's art

In his vastly productive, but tragically short, career Bonington created an art that was so distinctly personal that it seems to belong essentially to him and to manifest in every touch that quality of poetic refinement which was the natural basis of his style. When one thinks of him one thinks automatically of the subjects he painted with such brilliancy and feeling – the ports and shipping, the Normandy heath and coast scenes, and the ancient towns of France and Italy where brightly clothed figures glow out

River scene in Picardy. Water-colour. This drawing forms the basis of Bonington's oil painting of the same subject in the collection of Sir John Heathcoat Amory, Bt. (See colour section Plate 8.) 1822.

View on the Normandy coast. Oil. 1823-4.

between crumbling and leaning walls. His fondness for such things made him paint them with a freshness and richness of effect which startles us even today.

A large proportion of his work was in water-colour, and his command of the medium puts him among its greatest masters. Technically, he seems to have possessed from the start all the resources that gave his water-colours their particular clarity and brilliance. He knew, for example, how to use the paper surface to vary the texture of his washes; and he found that by dragging an almost dry brush over the paper he could give his colour a light, powdery quality. And, in his final years, he devised a method of glazing his water-colour shadows with a film of gum which gave them an

Landscape with cornfield. Water-colour. 1827.

added liquidity and depth.

In his lifetime, and indeed for the rest of the nineteenth century, a great number of French and English artists adopted Bonington's water-colour style and technique. Even in the work of the cosmopolitan Whistler one sees in his use of sharp, clear water-colour washes the influence of Bonington, though probably the influence was an unconscious one, derived at second-hand from the French. In fact, so many artists learnt from him in one way or another, artists who were versatile and accomplished in their own right, that one tends to forget that it was Bonington who was their initial inspiration. Indeed, it might be said of him that he constitutes a dividing point in the English water-colour tradition. If one takes Girtin as the main and original source, the artist to whom Constable, Turner and Bonington himself owed their beginnings, then one sees how radically Bonington diverged from the particular kind of naturalism which such artists as Constable, Cox and De Wint developed from their study of Girtin. As a general rule, these artists tended to see nature in terms of rounded masses, with green as the predominant tone, but, for Bonington, naturalism was less important than the life and atmosphere which an artist could create by the imaginative use of his technical resources. For him the paramount aim was clarity, delicacy of touch and brilliancy of tone. And it is in his water-colours, especially with their clear, sharp-edged washes, that he shows his originality, developing in them a style that was to form, even in his own short lifetime, the basis of a new tradition.

Delacroix once adjured artists to banish earth colours from their palettes; and in Bonington this same concern for pure and limpid tones leads him to refine on nature, so to speak, to create in his medium an atmospheric clarity that will bring out colour in its purest and most telling form. In his oils and in his water-colours this quality of tonal refinement is the essence of his style. In his oil paintings the silvery whiteness of his pigment, even when thickly applied, is always delicately luminous in its effect, and the masses in his composition seem to focus light rather than reduce it. Characteristically, too, the trees he paints are generally of a slender, feathery kind; a preference largely explained, one feels, by the fact that trees of this form cast less shadow, and their airy stems and branches easily fuse themselves into an expanse of luminous sky.

Sometimes, when influenced by Constable, Bonington paints darker and more broken skies; or, remembering Turner, he for once abandons his cool habitual tones to capture the glowing brilliance of a sunset. But, on the whole, his art remains consistently his own, personal in its subtle tonality and in its lucent, pearly freshness. In his figure subjects Bonington's debt to the Old Masters is plain enough, but in his coast scenes, his landscapes and his architectural studies the past hardly counts. From his first days in France these things must have impressed his consciousness profoundly and have determined in an almost compulsive way the form his art was to take.

With Bonington, it might be said, there was no experimental phase, no tentative beginnings. From the start he knew what to paint and he knew instinctively how to paint it. And, like the development of his talent, rewards and recognition came to him with a readiness that fate allows only to a chosen few. The youthful water-colours, exhibited with such effect in the windows of Paris art shops, testify to the appeal his work had from the beginning. And here, perhaps, it is relevant to remind ourselves that the impact of these water-colours was all the greater on account of their novelty. Not only, as we have already seen, was the use of water-colour new then to the French, but the subjects that Bonington was so adept in painting, port scenes and shipping pieces, were subjects which French artists themselves seem never to have attempted. In 1837, nearly ten years after Bonington's death, they were still a novelty in Paris, as William Callow tells us in his autobiography:

'I sent a water-colour drawing to a local Exhibition at Boulogne-sur-Mer, for which I was awarded a silver medal. I was principally painting sea-pieces at the time; they were quite a novelty in Paris, and I received many orders for them from Durand-Ruel.'

There is a story that it was the chance sight of a work by Bonington in a shop window which persuaded Corot to abandon a career in trade and devote himself to painting. The story is probably apocryphal, but the influence of Bonington on Corot's early work is indisputable. There are differences, of course, even when they seem closest in their style. Corot, in his wonderful early paintings, tends to be more rugged and classical than Bonington, but in his cool tonality and in the poetic quality of his light it is from the English artist that Corot basically derives. In this sense it might be claimed for Bonington that he was Corot's first and only master.[8]

Yet we must beware of overestimating Bonington's status in the history of art. He died too young for us to be certain that his immense promise would have fulfilled itself in an achievement comparable with Constable's or Turner's. As we see now, the truly original artists of the nineteenth century were those who had courage enough to tread a lonely and often ridiculed path. Was Bonington such a man? Would his growing interest in history and subject painting have proved fatal in the end, turning him utlimately into a mere virtuoso exponent of popular taste?

If such doubts occur, there is the actual achievement to set against them – the

The Abbey of St Armand, Rouen. Water-colour. 1827-8.

brilliant water-colours and the wonderful series of landscape and coast-scene paintings which display in style and feeling all the special qualities that the term 'Boningtonian' has come to imply. Though never the central figure in a movement, he created a style that echoes through the work of a succession of French and English artists. Even Turner himself may have owed something to Bonington for the breadth and poetical feeling which distinguish his own sea-pieces. In one case the debt is obvious, so much so that it seems to be intentionally stressed. In a painting *Calais Sands*,[9] exhibited two years after Bonington's death, Turner pays tribute to the dead artist's memory by overtly borrowing his style and by choosing a subject that is essentially Boningtonian. In this picture Turner has painted a long, receding stretch of beach on which a line of French fisherwomen bend over the wet sands as they dig for bait.

Normandy coast scene, low tide. Water-colour.

It is a hauntingly beautiful picture, as much Bonington as Turner; a unique combination of two of the most poetic sensibilities in English painting. And, in a way, it exemplifies the kind of influence Bonington exerted on other artists. It was never in his nature to be a revolutionary, though when his work first appeared in Paris, many of the old school regarded him as one. No, what he was remembered for after his death, and what his followers strove to emulate, was his technical facility, his personal style, his sensitive and poetical touch. This legacy, it might be said, was relatively unimportant and had little or no bearing on the major artistic developments which occurred after Bonington's death, particularly in France. But this is not wholly true. Through his influence on Corot and Delacroix – forerunners of the Impressionists and pioneers in the free use of light and colour – it can be claimed for Bonington (as it can for Constable and Turner) that he played an initiatory part in a movement that produced some of the greatest art of the nineteenth century.

As the names of Bonington and Delacroix are so often linked together, it is appropriate that the last word on Bonington should come from the great French painter who cherished the memory of his friend and fellow-artist to the end. In a note on Bonington, written for Théophile Thoré in 1861, Delacroix says:

'I could never weary of admiring his marvellous understanding of effects, and the facility of his execution; not that he was easily satisfied. On the contrary, he frequently repainted things that were completely finished and seemed wonderful to us; but his skill was such that his brush immediately produced fresh effects as delightful as the first. He turned to good account all sorts of details he had discovered in the works of the masters, and fitted them very skilfully into his own compositions. These include figures taken almost whole from paintings that were familiar to everybody, and it did not worry him in the least. This habit by no means detracts from the merit of his works; these details, taken, as it were, from life, and which he made his own (chiefly as regards the dress of his figures), enhanced their air of truthfulness and never smacked of pastiche . . . We all loved him. I used to say to him sometimes, "You are king in your own realm and Raphael could not have done what you do. Don't worry about other people's qualities or the proportions of their pictures since your own are masterpieces."'

[1] When the French dealers ceased buying his work, Constable lost not only an important source of income, but also the chance of establishing himself as an international figure. Had his paintings continued to sell in Paris, his own countrymen would undoubtedly have thought more highly of him

Landscape with a wagon. Oil. 1825.

and he would not have ended his days as a neglected, often ridiculed, artist. As his friend, John Fisher, once hopefully prophesied: 'English boobies, who dare not trust their own eyes, will discover your merits when they find you admired in Paris.'

[2] It was Dominic Colnaghi who advised Constable on the arrangements he should make with the French art dealer, Arrowsmith, the purchaser of *The Haywain* in 1824.

[3] In June, 1837, his remains were re-interred at Kensal Green Cemetery.

[4] On the day of Bonington's funeral Sir Thomas Lawrence wrote to Mrs Forster in Paris: 'Alas for Bonington! Your presage has been fatally verified; the last duties have been paid to him today. Except in the case of Mr Harlowe, I have never known in my own time the early death of talent so promising and so rapidly and obviously improving. If I may judge from the later direction of his studies and from remembrance of a morning's conversation, his mind seemed expanding every way, and ripening into full maturity of taste and elevated judgment, with that generous ambition which makes confinement to lesser departments in the art painfully irksome and annoying.'

[5] Another mistress shared by the two artists was the mysterious Madame Dalton, a young French dancer married to an Englishman. It is said that Bonington, when he felt that he was dying, bequeathed Madame Dalton to Delacroix as a kind of legacy.

[6] Now in La Bibliothèque d'Art and d'Archéologie, Paris.

[7] French sources have hinted that these letters were destroyed because they dealt too frankly with the subject of *amours*.

[8] Corot is reported to have once said that, unlike Delacroix, who had picked up the principles of art from other painters, he had learned nothing from anyone.

[9] Now in the Bury Art Gallery. When first exhibited at the Academy in 1830, Turner's description of the painting was: 'Calais sands, low water, *Poissards* collecting bait.'

5. BONINGTON'S LITHOGRAPHS

NO account of Bonington would be complete without some reference to his work in lithography, a form of art to which he made an important contribution. Delacroix admits that his own efforts in this field were inferior to Bonington's.

'My drawing is very far from having the delicacy of touch that he brought to his lithographs, and indeed to every product of his admirable talent.'

We do not know who taught Bonington lithography, but Delacroix himself may have given him the benefit of his own practical experience. Almost from the outset of his career, when this new process of reproduction was gaining popularity, Delacroix did lithographic work for the papers to keep himself financially afloat, even as early as 1820. For him, and for many other artists, this was only bread-and-butter hackwork, and it may possibly have prejudiced him against undertaking lithographic work with any degree of enthusiasm.[1] Or perhaps, as his tribute to Bonington's skill suggests, he was discouraged by a sense of his own technical deficiency, that lack of delicacy in his pencil touch to which he himself refers and which would have prevented him from achieving the subtle gradations of light and shade which Bonington's lithographs display.

The emphasis that Delacroix places here on delicacy of touch is a reminder of the

Dunkerque. Etching.

special qualities that the lithograph possesses. It is, it might be claimed, the most direct and personal method of artistic reproduction. Basically, the process of lithography hinges on the fact that oil and water do not mix. In this method of reproduction the subject to be printed is drawn with a crayon or greasy lithographic pencil on a smooth limestone surface that will readily absorb both grease and water. The stone is then sponged with water and a roller, coated with a stiff, greasy ink, is passed over the stone, with the result that the wet parts reject the ink and the parts drawn on by the lithographic pencil hold it. A sheet of paper is then placed on the stone and put through a press. The resulting impression reproduces the grainy texture of the stone and has a soft and velvety quality which gives the lithographic print its distinctive character.

Invented by the Bavarian, Senefelder, in 1796, the process was developed and improved over the years. Bonington's friend and fellow artist, Thomas Shotter Boys, for instance, added to its scope by the use of colour lithography. His set of lithographs entitled *Picturesque architecture in Paris, Ghent, Antwerp, Rouen,* which were issued in London in 1839, were the first original lithographs printed in colour to be published.

However, by the middle of the nineteenth century the artistic standards of the colour lithograph had sadly declined. Degraded and commercialised by the introduction of new methods, it seemed doomed never to attract serious artists again. But, as sometimes happens in such cases, a new figure emerges with the kind of dynamic talent that can transform and revitalise a seemingly dead tradition. In the case of the lithograph the saving genius was Toulouse-Lautrec whose lithographic posters inspired many of France's greatest contemporary painters to use the process for the reproduction of their art.

But this final flowering of the lithograph does not really concern us here. In Bonington's day, it must be remembered, the process was still in the early stages of its development, and though Bonington never explored the possibilities of colour as Boys did, he brought to this, then novel, medium all his qualities of poetry and dexterity.

It was in 1824, the year of Bonington's successful début at the Paris Salon and the award of a gold medal for the pictures he exhibited there, that his first lithographs were published under the title *Restes et Fragments d'Architecture du Moyen Age*, part of this work having been done in 1823. It was characteristic of Bonington, with his precocious gift for art, that he took this new venture completely in his stride and was master of its technique from the very start. Altogether, in the course of the next three years, he produced some sixty or so lithographs, mostly from his own composition, but also a number from the work of other artists, as in the case of his illustrations to

Tour du Gros Horloge à Evreux.
Lithograph. 1824.

Rue du Gros Horloge à Rouen. Lithograph. 1824.

Pernot's *Vues Pittoresques d'Écosse* (1826), to the *Voyage Pittoresque dans le Brésil* by Maurice Rugendas (1827), and to the *Contes du Gay Sçavoir*, published in 1828.

Of the other lithographs at least thirty-seven are original, or possibly forty-two, if we accept as original five of those in the Franche-Comté series. Four of these prints are dated in the underlines 1825; the question of their originality hinges on the possibility that Bonington made an unrecorded journey to the Franche-Comté country prior to his passing through it on his way to Italy in 1826. Such gaps in our knowledge are a reminder of the kind of problem that Bonington's short career poses for the art historian.

Thanks to the scholarly researches of Mr Atherton Curtis, we have now a complete and chronological list of Bonington's lithographs reproduced on page 000. To this list, published by Paul Prouté of Paris, has been added by way of preface, as Mr Curtis himself has done, a letter of Bonington's in Mr Curtis's possession which touches on the subject of the lithographs. Addressed to Bonington's friend, James Roberts, this hasty and informal letter (with a section added by Alexandre Colin) gives us a glimpse of that light-hearted side of Bonington's nature which made him the lively and stimulating companion *('ce luron-là')* that Delacroix remembered with affection all his life. The spelling is Bonington's own.

'Dunkerque Fev 1824

'Mon cher Ami,

'We have taken a room here for 15 days it was nice & clean when we entered but however it is somewhat changed since then, as for he does not even know how to put a thing buy after him – see what it is to have a wife – lets the fire go out – loses himself – spils the lamp oil &&.

'Je demande la plume a Bonnington pour vous dire deux mots, mon cher Roberts. C'est que j'ai bien du regret que nous ne puissions etre avec vous ici, notre plaisir serait. double si nous pouvions le partager avec vous, nous parlons bien souvent de vous, mais ce n'est pas la même chose que si nous vous avions la, quand je fais quelque maladresse, bonington me dit aussitôt, si tu voyais comme Roberts se tirerait de là, et j'en suis bien convaincu quoique je n'aye pas encore pu me procurer le plaisir de voyager avec vous, mais patience, j'espère que je ne perdrai pas pour attendre, en attendant ce moment désiré, agréez je vous prie les sentiments sincères de l'amitié dont je me suis senti pénétré pour vous depuis le moment que j'ai en l'avantage de vous connaître et vêuillez présenter a Madame Roberts mes hommages respectueux. votre tout devoué Colin.

'C'est a l'occasion du Carnaval auquel nous avions assisté aujourdhui que je reprend ma lettre interrompue depuis hier soir figurez vous mon ami que le Carnaval de Paris n'est que de la St Jean aupres de celui ci nous avons vu une mexicaine ou tous les bouchers de la Ville ont rempli les roles des caciques. J'espere vous en envoyer une echantillon a fin de ma lettre si ma memoire est suffisante – le droit du masque vous donne ici la femme a discretion comme du pain chez la restauranteur . . . pour embrasser seulement mais beaucoup de ces dames courent les rues expres – Mon ami Colin travaille bien mais dans des crispations eternelles Je mange pour nous deux, & je vous souhaite une sante aussi bonne que la mienne Je finis ma lettre dans la crainte de ne pouvoir donner un portrait assez ample de la scène d'aujourdhui veuillez a Mme Roberts mes hommages respectueux & croyez a l'amitié sincere de votre

'affectioné
'R. P. Bonington'

'ecrivez moi de suite poste restante a Dunkerque.

'I should be glad to know how feillet[2] has printed my other stones;[3] or if you have heard anything respecting the putting off of the exhibition – but however any news will be acceptable – I hope to hear that Mrs Roberts is better – pray let me know if you have heard anything of Ensom Mon cher je suis au desespoir, je ne fait que grater – dis moi quand vous serez disponible que je puisse m'arranger to meet you remember me a tout le monde.'

[1] Actually Delacroix produced about a hundred lithographs.
[2] Feillet, lithographic printer.
[3] The stones about which Bonington asks for news are those done for the series *Restes et Fragments d'Architecture du Moyen Age*.

1 Dunkerque

RESTES ET FRAGMENTS D'ARCHITECTURE

2 Restes Gothiques
3 Architecture du Moyen Age.
4 Hospice de Charité.
5 Abbeville—Vue prise de la route de Calais.
6 Beauvais—Intérieur d'une Cour.
7 Bergues—La tour du Marché.
8 Caen—Église Saint Sauveur.
9 Caen—Maison Grande Rue Saint—Pierre.
10 Lillebonne—Château d'Harcourt.
11 Rouen—Cathédrale Notre-Dame.
12 Rouen—Entrée de la Salle des Pas-Perdus, Palais de Justice.
13 Rouen—Fontaine de la Crosse.
14 Abbeville—Porte de l'église Saint Wulfran.
15 Le Matin
16 Porte d'une Maison en bois du XVe Siècle.

NORMANDIE (VOYAGES PITTORESQUE)

17 Rue du Gros—Horloge, Rouen.
18 Élise de Saint--Gervais et Saint-Protais à Gisors.
19 Tour aux Archives à Vernon.
20 Tour du Gros-Horlage, Évreux.
21 Élise de Saint—Taurin, Évreux (cul-de-lampe).

FRANCHE-COMTE (VOYAGES PITTORESQUE)

22 Pesmes
23 Église de l'Abbaye de Tournus.
24 Facade de l'église de Brou.
25 Tombeau de Marguerite de Bourbon, Église de Brou.
26 Pierre de Vaivre.
27 Croix de Moulin—les—Planches.
28 Vue générale des ruines du Château d'Arlay.
29 Ruines du Château d'Arlay. 1er planche.
30 Ruines du Château d'Arlay. 2e planche.
31 Vue d'une rue des faubourgs de Besan*on.

VUES DE L'ÉCOSSE

32 Édimbourg vu de la Chappelle Saint Antoine.
33 Édimbourg vu du Calton Hill.
34 Ancienne porte à Stirling.
35 Château de Dounc.
36 Lac de Killin. Loch Tay.
37 Brackline.
38 Glenfinlas.
39 Lac Lomond.
40 Château d'Argyle.
41 Château de Bothwell.
42 Ancienne tour près de Lanark.
43 Les Pendus—The Escape from Argyle Castle.
44 Le Duel—A Duel between Frank & Rashleigh (Rob Roy).

CAHIER DE SIX SUJETS

45 Le Repos.
46 La Prière.
47 La Conversation.
48 Le Silence favorable.
49 Les Plaisirs paternels.
50 Le Retour.

VOYAGE DANS LE BRÉSIL

51 Campos sur les bords du Rio das Velhas.
52 Entrée de la rade de Rio Janeiro.
53 Embouchure de la rivière Caxoera.

54 Secours Aux Naufragés (Manby life-saving apparatus in use).

CONTES DU GAY SÇAVOIR (IMITATION OF MEDIAEVAL ILLUMINATED STYLE).

55 Titre.
56 De la Dame de la belle Sagesse.
57 Du Sacristain de Saint Amgadresme.
58 De la Dame sans merci.
59 Du Braconnier.
60 La veillée des Fileuses.
61 De Jouvencel qui se Marie à Madame Marie. Mère de Dieu.

BIBLIOGRAPHY

Arnold's Magazine of Fine Arts, new series III, London, 1833-34
L'Art, Paris, 1879
Art Journal, London, 1856
L'Artiste, Paris, 1837, 1848, 1857, 1886
La Belle Assemblée, London, 1826
Beraldi, *Les Graveurs du XIXe Siècle*, Paris
Binyon, L., *English Watercolour*, London, 1933
La Biographie Michaud, Paris
Biographie Rabbe (Supplement), Paris
Blanc, Charles, *Histoire des Peintres de toutes Écoles*, Paris, 1863
Bouvenne, A., *Catalogue de l'Oeuvre gravé et lithographié de R. P. Bonington*, Paris, 1873
Burlington Magazine, vols 11, 12, 51, 71, London
Callow, William, *Autobiography*, ed. H. M. Cundall, London, 1908
Champlin, John Denison and Perkins, Charles C., *Cyclopaedia of Painters and paintings*, Paris, 1969
Chesneau, E., *La Peinture Anglaise*, Paris
The Connoisseur, vols 9, 10, 67, 88, 93, 98, London
Curtis, Atherton, *Catalogue de l'oeuvre lithographié et gravé de R. P. Bonington*, Paris, 1939
Cundall, H. M., *History of British Watercolour*, London, 1929
Cunningham, Allan, *Lives of the British Painters*, 3 vols, London, 1880
Dictionary of National Biography
Dubuisson, A., 'Bonington et l'influence de l'école anglaise sur la peinture de paysage en France', *Walpole Society*, 1912-13
Dubuisson, A. and Hughes, C. E., *Richard Parkes Bonington: his life and work*, London, 1924
Encyclopaedia Britannica
Eschollier, Raymond, *Delacroix*, Paris, 1930
Fontainas, André, *Histoire de la Peinture Française du XIXe Siècle*
Friedlander, W., *David to Delacroix*, Cambridge, Mass., 1952
Frantz, Henri, 'The Art of Richard Parkes Bonington', *The Studio*, 1904
Gazette des Beaux Arts, Paris, 1859, 1876
Gauthier, M., *La vie et l'art romantiques*, 1945
Gautier, T., *Tableaux à la plume*
'Exposition de 1860', *Gazette des Beaux Arts*, 1860, vol. 5
Gentleman's Magazine, vol. 98
Gigoux, Jean, *Causeries sur les Artistes de mon Temps*, Paris, 1885

Le Globe, Paris, 1828
Grundy, C. R., *Catalogue of the pictures in the collection of Frederick John Nettlefold,* 1933
Hamilton, G., *École Anglaise,* 1831-32
Harding, J. D., *A series of subjects from the works of the late R. P. Bonington; drawn on stone by J. D. Harding*, London, 1829-30
Hediard, Germain, *Lithographies de Bonington*, Paris
Hénon, *L'Industrie des tulles et dentelles mécaniques dans le département du Pas de Calais, 1815-1900*, 1900
Holme, C. and Wedmore, Sir F., *English Watercolour*, London, 1900
Huet, René Paul, *Paul Huet d'après ses notes, sa correspondence, ses contemporains*, Paris, 1911
Hughes, C. E., 'Notes on Bonington's Parents', *Walpole Society,* vol. III, 1914
Ilchester, the Earl of, *Chronicles of Holland House*, London, 1820-1900
Jal, A., *Esquisses, croquis, pochades sur le Salon de 1827,* Paris
Jameson, Mrs, *Companion to the most celebrated private galleries of art,* 1844
Joets, Jules, *L'école des Beaux Arts de St Omer*, St Omer, 1909
Joubin, André, *Correspondence Generale d'Eugène Delacroix,* Paris, 1936-38
Le Journal d'Eugène Delacroix, Paris, 1932
Lanson, René, *Le gout du Moyen Age en France au XVIIIe siècle,* 1926
Layard, G. S., *Sir Thomas Lawrence's Letter-bag*, London, 1905
Le Franc, J. Tripier, *Histoire de la Vie et la Mort du Baron Gros,* Paris, 1880
Lemonnier, *Gros,* 1905
Library of Fine Arts, London, 1832
Literary Gazette, London, 1826, 1828, 1832
Literary Souvenir, London, 1835
London Magazine, London, 1829
London Weekly Review, London, 1828-29
Magazine of Fine Arts, London, 1833
Mercure de France, Paris, 1901
Miquel, Pierre, *Paul Huet,* Sceaux, 1962
Le Musée Artistique et Literaire, Paris, 1881
Nagler, *Neues Allgemeines Kunstler-Léxicon,* Berlin
New Monthly Magazine, London, 1828, 1829, 1834
Notes and Queries, 4th Series, VII, pp. 502-3, London
La Nouvelle Biographie Generale Firmin Didot, Paris, 1862
Portfolio, London, 1881

Raffaelli, J. F., *Promenades d'un artiste au Musée du Louvre,*
Redgrave, R. *Dictionary of the English School,* London, 1874
Watercolour Painting in England, London, 1878
Reau, L., *L'ère romantique,* 1949
Revue Britannique, Paris, 1833
Revue de L'Art Ancienne et Moderne, Paris, 1909
Roget, J. L., *History of the Old Water-Colour Society,* London, 1891
Rosenthal, *La Peinture Romantique,* Paris
Roundell, James, *Thomas Shotter Boys,* London, 1974
Ryley, S. W., *The Intinerant, or Memoirs of an Actor,* vol. VI, 1817
Shirley, The Hon. Andrew (ed.), *Leslie's Memoirs of the life of Constable,* London, 1937
Bonington, London, 1941
Spencer, Marion, *Catalogue of Bonington Exhibition, Nottingham,* 1965
Stewart, Jean, *Delacroix. Selected Letters,* London, 1971
Stokes, Hugh, *Girtin and Bonington,* London, 1922
The Studio, London, 1904
Taylor, Baron, *Voyages Pittoresques dans l'ancienne France,* Paris, 1823-47
Taylor, Basil, *Mellon collection catalogue of English painting,* Virginia, 1963
Thornton Society's Transactions, 1910
Walpole Society, Journal II
Wellington, Hubert, *Journal of Eugène Delacroix,* London, 1951
Whitley, W. T., *Art in England, 1820-37,* London, 1930
Whitman, A. C., *S. W. Reynolds,* London, 1903
Willemin, *Monuments français inédits pour servir a l'histoire des arts,* 1808-39

INDEX